T0328576

Cambridge Elements ≡

Elements in Defence Economics
edited by
Keith Hartley
University of York

BRITAIN AND THE POLITICAL ECONOMY OF EUROPEAN MILITARY AEROSPACE COLLABORATION, 1960–2023

Keith Hayward
Fellow of the Royal Aeronautical Society

CAMBRIDGE
UNIVERSITY PRESS

CAMBRIDGE
UNIVERSITY PRESS

Shaftesbury Road, Cambridge CB2 8EA, United Kingdom

One Liberty Plaza, 20th Floor, New York, NY 10006, USA

477 Williamstown Road, Port Melbourne, VIC 3207, Australia

314–321, 3rd Floor, Plot 3, Splendor Forum, Jasola District Centre,
New Delhi – 110025, India

103 Penang Road, #05–06/07, Visioncrest Commercial, Singapore 238467

Cambridge University Press is part of Cambridge University Press & Assessment,
a department of the University of Cambridge.

We share the University's mission to contribute to society through the pursuit of
education, learning and research at the highest international levels of excellence.

www.cambridge.org
Information on this title: www.cambridge.org/9781009291859
DOI: 10.1017/9781009291873

First published 2023

A catalogue record for this publication is available from the British Library.

ISBN 978-1-009-29185-9 Paperback
ISSN 2632-332X (online)
ISSN 2632-3311 (print)

Britain and the Political Economy of European Military Aerospace Collaboration, 1960–2023

Elements in Defence Economics

DOI: 10.1017/9781009291873
First published online: June 2023

Keith Hayward
Fellow of the Royal Aeronautical Society

Author for correspondence: Keith Hayward, Keith.hayward48@btinternet.com

Abstract: The United Kingdom has been collaborating with international, primarily European, partners in the design, development and production of advanced combat aircraft for over sixty years. Driven by a combination of rising costs and limited domestic markets, collaboration has also been a highly political act involving a combination of national, industrial and technological interests. Over the years, the form of collaboration has evolved, in some cases leading to the creation of transnational companies. The United Kingdom has been a pioneer of globalisation in the defence industry, establishing a strong presence inside the US defence market and has become a significant partner with American companies in key military aerospace programmes. This has contributed to divisions within the European military aerospace industry which are likely to continue into the next generation of combat aircraft.

Keywords: defence spending, military aircraft, aerospace industry, political economy, Anglo-European relations

JEL classifications: F23, F50, H56, L64

ISBNs: 9781009291859 (PB), 9781009291873 (OC)
ISSNs: 2632-332X (online), 2632-3311 (print)

Contents

Introduction

The practice of European aerospace collaboration is now over sixty years old and Britain's involvement with its neighbours, if dated from the Anglo-French Concorde Treaty of November 1962, almost exactly that. On a personal note, my first tentative essay on the subject dates from 1969; as an undergraduate student of Defence Analysis, I considered the 'pros and cons' of European military aerospace collaboration. It would be fun, if somewhat trite, to write that nothing much has changed in the interim. While there is an element of deja vu in this Element, much has changed from the 1960s. My naïf essay appeared at a time when the some of the first collaborative programmes had either collapsed or were in trouble (I should also admit that my first published article on the Airbus from 1976 was less than hopeful about its future). From the perspective of the second quarter of the twenty-first century Europe now has several world-class trans-European defence/aerospace companies – at least three of which are better described as global in scale and scope, and two of these are British owned and headquartered. The United States still dominates much of the world defence industry and export markets, but in some areas of advanced military technology Europe has at least stayed in touch with the Americans – something that would not have been confidently predicted fifty years ago.

From a more parochial British viewpoint, by the early 1960s, the UK aerospace industry was, as I have written elsewhere, *Struggling to Survive.*[1] A belated rationalisation of the leading companies had produced two still under-resourced airframe groups, British Aircraft Corporation (BAC) and HSA, one helicopter firm, Westland, and two engine suppliers, Rolls-Royce and Bristol Siddeley Engines (BSE), the former more successful and capable than the latter, indeed perhaps the only truly world-class company in the national industry. The creation of two competing aircraft and engine companies was explicitly aimed at maintaining some degree of domestic competition, but which in practice only led to an implicit 'Buggins Turn' in allocating government-funded work. In 1966, Rolls unilaterally ended this charade by taking over BSE. The 1950s had seen the delivery of many British military programmes, few of which in the later years of the decade had made much headway in world markets; some had been absolute turkeys. The French, especially Dassault's family of fighters, had begun to pull ahead and the Swedes had begun to deliver some very effective products. Other Europeans, primarily Germany and Italy, were beginning to rebuild their aerospace industries. The Americans, however, were the main source of supply to the NATO alliance and other 'allied' nations.

---

[1] Forthcoming.

Worse was to come – in 1964–5, the newly elected Labour government axed a series of military aircraft projects, including the white hope BAC TSR.2. To rub salt in the wound, the government then ordered American aircraft to fill the bomber and transport gap left by these cuts. To balance some of the lost work, Labour continued with the expensive 'Anglicised' American F-4 K Phantom and somewhat reluctantly funded Hawker's VSTOL P.1127, later known as the Harrier. However, the aerospace industry, although much maligned by Labour politicians, was still seen as a key employer and a high-value technology-intensive sector. This implied the need for continued support either in the form of R&D funding launch aid for civil projects or military contracts. The struggle to sustain the industry on the back of a small domestic market against a background of rapidly escalating development costs was the main reason the TSR.2 was axed and why the Labour government picked up the thread of cooperation with the French.[2] Matters were not helped by the tendency on the part of the RAF and MoD to ignore the export potential in formulating require-ments, a British failing that continued for decades after the war. The United Kingdom also cancelled projects, such as the supersonic Hunter, that might have won a share of the world market. The French, on the other hand, would tend to prioritise a wider marketability – a factor that helped to explain sales of Dassault aircraft.[3]

The 1962 Concorde treaty hopefully signalled a better way: share the devel-opment costs and launch projects between two comparable states and launch production on the basis of a wider 'domestic' market. With the publication of the Plowden Report in 1965 into the UK aircraft industry, the Labour govern-ment went further, stating categorically that the United Kingdom should never again independently build large and complex aircraft, civil or military. So, building on the Concorde principle (no matter that Labour also wanted to cancel this project as well as the others in the 1964–5 cull), by 1966, the United Kingdom was committed to a series of bilateral military joint projects with France.

This Element begins at this point, describing what would turn out to be decades of turbulent politics and perhaps some dubious defence economics. It finishes with a much stronger British military aerospace industry, but with unfinished European business. Where possible (which effectively means up to the mid-1990s) I have used UK government archives located at Kew as well as some unpublished sources located at the National Aerospace Library (NAL) in

---

[2] The economic rationale for the TSR-2 cancellation might have been more justifiable had the decision not also included an order for the American F-111, which was itself cancelled in 1967.

[3] I am grateful to Mr Paul Stoddard for this observation, and for several other comments on an earlier draft of this Element.

Farnborough.[4] This is still only a partial survey of original sources and events are largely from a British perspective (although I am grateful from comments by my colleagues in the French Air and Space Academy). However, using archival sources even to this point introduces a vital contemporary historical voice to the political-economic analysis of what remains a continuing issue in Anglo-European defence industrial relations.

Although the approach is primarily historical, focusing on the political context of the primary military aircraft collaborative programmes, economic factors are never too far from the surface. These include the effects of scope/scale economies, cost escalation and supply chain issues that shaped the motivation for and operation of the programmes considered in the narrative. The former is of particular significance, as the United Kingdom and other leading European aerospace powers sought to create and to maintain an *affordable* national or shared capability that could aspire to world-class standards, which in practice meant US standards. Similarly, although the subject matter is defined by the *aircraft systems* developed in Europe between 1960 and 2024, the importance of key suppliers, particularly in the engine and avionics sectors, was frequently a decisive element in the interplay of national industrial interests.

Finally, while military aerospace is central to this analysis, some mention is made of civil aerospace and the emergence of a competitive family of airliners developed and built by the Airbus consortium, in which the industries of Britain, France and Germany, the *'big three'* players in the European aerospace industry, integrated their national industries successfully to challenge the United States. This history was not without links to military developments, particularly in the Anglo-French rivalries in the engine sector played out in both the story of Airbus and at least two of the major military programmes discussed in Section 1. The failure to establish a 'military Airbus' is perhaps one of the great 'what ifs?' of the history of European aerospace collaboration.[5]

There is certainly scope for a more diligent (and younger) analyst to continue this work, expanding perhaps on the wider defence industrial context beyond

---

[4] Of particular value were the diaries of Freddie Page, who was closely involved in several key post-1945 military aerospace programmes, including collaborative projects up to the late 1970s. His diaries are kept at the NAL, but I also prepared a paper based on his memories for the Royal Aeronautical Society; Keith Hayward, *Freddie Page; Aerospace Engineer and Businessman; The life and times of Sir Frederick Page, CBE, MA, FEng, Hon. FRAeS,* RAeS Paper, 2013.

[5] The political history of the Airbus is a complex and fascinating study in its own right, particularly the role of successive British governments in nearly derailing the rise of Airbus on at least three occasions. For an archive-based study of two of these near disasters for European aerospace, see Keith Hayward, 'Airbus Industrie, Britain's Return', *The Aviation Historian,* Issue No. 38, January 2022, pp. 10–18 and 'Britain's Aerospace Brexit', *The Aviation Historian,* Issue 28, July 2019, pp. 10–19

the narrow confines of military aerospace. But focusing on the single sector that pioneered and still dominates the universe of collaborative defence projects remains a valid approach, and the historical approach validated by the fact that much of the present reflects an unbroken stream of cause and effect.

As the United Kingdom moves into the unexplored bourn that is Brexit, the lessons of the past half decade or more should be obvious. Losing contact with the European market and perhaps drifting away from our industrial neighbours across the Channel could pose a serious challenge to the long-term health of the UK defence aerospace industry. The growing integration of European R&D and its closure to UK-based actors is a sign of things to come. Links with the United States, although more than a little tempting, will continue to threaten dependency and exclusion from what a friend and colleague in the industry has called the 'noble aspects' of development – systems integration and the acquiring the core technology of systems design and development.[6] Forging alternative alliances across the world may come to fill some of this prospective gap, but they have yet to be proven and tested by political or economic crises. As the reader will discover, these tests can be to the destruction of collaborative hopes and aspirations. The period covers what might be described in retrospect as the era of 'project-based' European collaboration involving British aerospace companies that started in the early 1960s as a bilateral phenomenon, expanding into a more multilateral basis and concluding to date, in the early 2020s, as a more globalised process. This Element may thus act as a primer for the twists and turns of launching and managing over time a complex collaborative defence–industrial relationship. At the very least the story is rarely without interest.

European states have been collaborating on successive generations of military aircraft since the late 1950s, but with increasing intensity from the mid-1960s. The economic rationale for this activity has been well covered by several authors. In practice, collaboration has also been a complex political exercise involving a mixture of national military, but perhaps often more decisively, vital industrial and technological interests. Although European military aerospace collaboration has included most of the major European aerospace companies, the core actors have been the United Kingdom, France and Germany. The interplay of this triad has shaped most of the key aircraft projects: the Transall (1960), the Jaguar and AFVG, (1966), Alpha Jet (1974) MRCA/Tornado, (1968), EFA/Rafale (1985), A400 M (1990) and into the current negotiations concerning advanced drones and a further generation of combat aircraft. There has also been a parallel evolution of European rotary aircraft collaboration and

---

[6] Air Marshall, Sir Brian Burridge, also formerly of Finmeccanica and CEO Royal Aeronautical Society.

joint work on guided weapons. Collaboration has not been exclusively European; the United Kingdom in particular has worked with the United States on the AV-8B Harrier (1976), the T-45 Goshawk (1981) and along with several other European states, the F-35 Lightning II (2001). But the United Kingdom has clearly been at the heart of European military aerospace cooperation since the early 1960s. (See Table 1 for the main UK collaborative programmes.)

Collaboration has been driven by a mixture of hard economics and political interest. The former was characterised by the rapidly rising costs of developing advanced military aircraft and airliners and the difficulty of sustaining production on the back of a small domestic market. This increased the unit costs of production to an unaffordable level, undermining both domestic affordability and attractiveness in export markets. Although collaboration increased administrative overheads, particularly when associated with inefficient but politically essential work-sharing practices, in splitting launch costs and increasing the base market the hope was to retain, at the 'cost' of some degree of lost autonomy, the greater part of a vital national technological and industrial capability. Politically, the United Kingdom sought to sustain close links with allies, especially in the context of seeking and then re-enforcing membership of the European Economic Union (EU), formally the European Economic Community (EEC).

This did not preclude cooperation with others, primarily the United States for specific projects. In some respects, the United Kingdom has thus managed to build effective alliances with both the United States and Europe. This has several related reasons. There are historical links stretching back to the Second World War, when the United Kingdom transferred critical military technologies to the United States, including early work on atomic weapons, radar and the jet engine. The combination of the Rolls-Royce Merlin engine and the North American P-45 airframe on a British initiative turned a mediocre aircraft into one of the war's most successful combat aircraft. After the war the nuclear links were restored and became fundamental to UK security policies. Periodically, the United Kingdom has produced unique designs that filled gaps in the US inventory – the Canberra bomber in the 1950s, the Harrier AV8B, which was much improved by, thanks to, American funding, and the Hawk trainer adopted by the US Navy as the Goshawk. Coming the other way, the United Kingdom has been prepared to buy or licence to build American aircraft such as the Apache attack helicopter.

As we will consider in Section 2, latterly the Anglo-American linkage has evolved into a more complex relationship based on investment inside their respective domestic defence markets. The United Kingdom in particular has

Table 1 UK aircraft collaborative programmes – 1962–2022

Date	Name	Function	Countries	Comments
1962	Concorde	Civil airliner	UK, Fr	Treaty based
1965	Jaguar	Fighter	UK, Fr	Bilateral consortium
1965	AFVG	Fighter	UK, Fr	Cancelled 1967
1967	Airbus A300	Civil airliner	UK, Fr, Ge	MoU UK leaves 1969
1968	MRCA/Tornado	Fighter	UK, Fr, Ge, It	MoU consortium
1975	AV–8B Harrier 11	VSTOL fighter	UK, US	US-led original UK design
1978	Airbus A310	Civil airliner	UK, Fr, Ge, Sp, Ne	UK rejoins consortium
1978	P110	Agile fighter	UK led Arab coalition	Discontinued 1982
1985	Eurofighter/Typhoon	Agile fighter	UK, Ge, It, Sp	Multilateral consortium
1994	A400 M	Military transport	UK, Fr, Ge, It, Sp,	Originally FIMA, 1982
2001	F–35 Lightning II (A, B & C)	Fighter bomber	US, UK, It, and others	In production
2022	Tempest	New-generation fighter	UK, It, Jap + Swe	Development phase
2022	FCAS	New-generation fighter	Fr, Ge	Development phase

placed fewer barriers to its defence market and industry than any other of the major NATO defence industrial powers. The United Kingdom has also been able to negotiate a less rigorous application of US technology transfer controls. The F-35 may in this light be seen as the peak of an Anglo-American collaborative stream. The United Kingdom is the only 'Tier One' partner, with privileged access to US-developed technology reciprocating (for the F-35B) with unique VSTOL engine capability as well as BAe Systems' (BAES) experience of 'lean manufacturing' applications in aerospace production. Finally, although the United Kingdom has from time to time shared with its European neighbours some fear of long-term dependence on the United States, the threat has seemed less intense seen from London than Paris.[7]

This Element's primary theme is the interplay of these economic, strategic and essentially political considerations. Although international collaboration could be suboptimal in terms of strict economic outcomes, the political returns and more pertinently in terms of sustaining the UK military aerospace industry, the exercise must on balance be described as a successful policy outcome.

Military aerospace has not been alone in exhibiting increases in intergenerational costs that have placed a growing burden on national defence equipment budgets. However, aerospace was the first to exhibit these effects and over the decades with increasing degrees of severity. This is largely due to the intrinsic complexity of advanced military aerospace across the board of aerodynamics, structures, propulsion and above all electronics. Land systems, although showing some degree of additional technological complexity and hence cost from one generation to the next, have been largely sustainable on the back of domestic orders. Naval systems – ships – have had the same relatively slower cost/complexity growth rate. Equally, much of the cost of larger vessels is bound up with the construction and integration of a very small number of ships. Combined with the often particularly high political salience of shipbuilding locations, the incentive and desirability to collaborate has been low.[8] In the case of submarines, especially nuclear, the value of strategic autonomy has also driven national construction. There are now more examples of cross-border naval and land systems collaboration, but aerospace remains the primary focus for international development.

---

[7] These fears have been more intense in the civil sector, but even here Rolls-Royce frequently saw the American market as paramount, and in 1978, the British government favoured links with Boeing or McDonnel Douglas over rejoining Airbus.

[8] Regional employment issues were also factors in the aerospace industry, such as the priority afforded to allocating work to Shorts of Northern Ireland, but such concerns weighed especially heavily in the shipbuilding sector.

But collaboration with whom? Working with the Europeans was not inevitable. However, in the 1950s and even into the last quarter of the twentieth century there were few realistic options. There were only a limited number of countries with either the defence budgets or the industrial capabilities with whom to collaborate effectively. Japan into the 1970s would fall into this category, but its own strong preferences were to work with American companies. In the 1950s, the United Kingdom had some links with the United States through trans-Atlantic licence-built production (the Canberra bomber for the USAF and Westland helicopters for the British Navy and other customers), and of course increasingly close nuclear weapons cooperation. However, in terms of establishing an egalitarian relationship that would support UK aerospace companies, the United States would be a problematic potential partner. This was in fact driven home when the United Kingdom contemplated the launch of a supersonic airliner: diverging technical and industrial interests forced the United Kingdom to look across the Channel for a partner. Working entirely with the Americans threatened to undermine domestic competence, and it was feared to ultimately drive up the costs of weapons procurement should the United Kingdom become dependent on the United States. The United Kingdom would later establish a deeper defence aerospace industrial relationship with the United States, which in later years contributed to the divisions and fractures in the European military aerospace sector, especially in advanced combat aircraft systems. While the United Kingdom has not been alone in looking to the United States for partners and off-the-shelf equipment in competition with European products, the depth and scale of the Anglo-American linkage represents a distinct alternative to a wholly European defence industrial policy.

What became the Concorde was also the first example of the link between industrial cooperation and wider European interests, linked to Britain's first unsuccessful attempt to join the EEC. The first steps in UK military aerospace cooperation would also be with France, but as Germany and Italy were rapidly remerging as aerospace manufacturing centres, they would quickly provide alternative partners for the United Kingdom. However, what would soon emerge as a problematic relationship with France helped to shape the strategic direction of the UK and European military aerospace industries. There is here a story of what did not happen: the formation of a permanent industrial structure comparable to the European Airbus, integrating the major European military aerospace companies, the better to challenge the United States in world markets and to develop projects more efficiently and economically. This is primarily the failure of France and the United Kingdom to agree on long-term industrial cooperation, largely due to the irreconcilable interests of their respective engine and aircraft companies. The role of Germany from the early 1960s and frequently into the 1980s was primarily a 'balancing', but not always easy collaborative partner in the Anglo-French dyad. Italy has also played a junior role in shaping these events, as does Sweden.

As already noted, a second theme, evident in the early 1970s, is the prospect of closer defence industrial ties with the United States, which would become a major theme of the 1990s, with two strands: project-based cooperation on the US F-35, which has de facto emerged as an alternative to all-European cooperation; and the globalisation of mainly, but not exclusively, Anglo-American companies, such as Rolls-Royce, BAe, Raytheon and General Electric from the mid-1990s.

Finally, there is the strand of increasing industrial integration in some aspects of European military aerospace, primarily in rotary craft with the emergence of two transnational companies Airbus Defence and Space and Leonardo, and in the guided weapons sector, a dominant Anglo-French-German entity in MBDA.

This Element is presented in three sections.

(1) A history of European cooperation in the development of high-value combat aircraft, beginning in the 1960s with the Anglo-French military aircraft package and the MRCA/Tornado programme. This era saw the emergence of a fundamental split in the European military aerospace sector – a schism reinforced by the failure of the five-nation European Fighter Aircraft (EFA) projects and the launch of competing French Rafale and the four-nation Eurofighter/Typhoon in the 1980s.

(2) The emergence of transnational European aerospace/defence companies. This section focuses on the creation of BAES and the growth of an Anglo-American axis in core military aerospace programmes, counterbalanced by largely European helicopter and missile multinational companies from the mid-1990s to the present.

(3) The Element ends with an examination of the current status of the European military aerospace sector; the continuing reverberations of Anglo-French differences over next-generation fighter programmes and the emergence of two competing projects. The conclusions are, from a European perspective, rather negative, or at least pessimistic about the future for a more integrated and thus potentially more efficient and effective UK military aerospace industrial base. From a purely British perspective, the future might be more promising.

1 Military Aerospace Collaboration 1960–1990

Launching Collaboration

In the early 1960s, the leading European aerospace nations – Britain, France, Germany and Italy – were at different stages in their post-war development. The UK industry was arguably the largest and most capable of the three, but by the early 1960s it was failing commercially, if not technically. France, on the other hand, was beginning to make significant inroads into world markets, especially in the military sector. Germany was at the early stages of a state-led recovery from the 1945–55 prohibitions on aerospace activity, but already with ambitions to do more than licence-build foreign designs. Italy was a little ahead of Germany in terms of indigenous capabilities, but with less motivation to acquire a world-class aerospace industry. Sweden was an outlier, with a highly capable military aerospace industry, selectively using imported technology to build an impressive range of fighter aircraft. But its neutrality-driven policies blocked formal collaboration with its European neighbours.

The United Kingdom

Despite a considerable investment in civil and military aircraft since 1945, by 1964, the UK aerospace industry was at a crossroads. Except for the Vickers Viscount, British civil programmes had failed miserably in world markets. On the military side, only the Hawker Hunter of the second generation of jet fighters was an unequivocal success. The three 'V' Bombers were at the heart of Britain's strategic nuclear force, technically successful but already obsolete, and, of course, unavailable as exports. An attempt to develop an indigenous ballistic missile, the Blue Streak, despite American help, had been expensively cancelled in 1960 as a military programme, although by 1962 it had become the first stage of a European satellite launcher. British carrier-based aircraft were outpaced by American products and obsolete by world standards (the NA39 Blackburn Buccaneer was something of an exception to this rule). The government-encouraged rationalisation of industry, initiated in 1959, had produced two competing aircraft and engine groups and one helicopter company. British Aircraft Corporation and HSA, although stronger than the fragmented industry of the 1950s, were still small by comparison with their American competitors. Ostensibly designed to compete for government work, both tended to receive contracts in turn. Rolls-Royce dominated its smaller competitor, BSE, and was by far the one UK aerospace company recognisably world class. This disparity, and consequent weight in government thinking towards the industry, would become even more evident with its take over of BSE in 1966, and the breakdown of merger talks between the BAC and Hawker Siddeley Aviation (HAS). Westland, the single helicopter company, had, contrary to government policy, built a solid basis on the back of licence-built US designs, but was now looking to develop its own designs.

The TSR.2 bomber programme exposed Britain's limitations as a major aerospace producer. Hugely ambitious in terms of strategic and tactical requirements and pushing the technical state of the art, the TSR.2 had been under development since the late 1950s as a joint BAC-HSA programme. It had been beset by continual changes in specification, rivalries between the two lead contractors, and overseen by a cumbersome procurement system. By 1964, although close to its first flight, it was far from fully proving its complex navigation and attack systems and was already late and far more expensive than originally estimated. The Conservative government in power since 1951 had already reversed its missile-based strategy announced in 1957; the TSR.2 was one of several advanced military designs under development, including the supersonic VSTOL HS P.1154 and HS 618 VSTOL transport. But as a programme, it already looked overambitious, too ambitious, given the development resources the United Kingdom possessed. Indeed, along with the P1154 and HS 681, curbing 'wasteful' defence projects such as the TSR-2 was a central feature of the Labour Opposition's 1964 election campaign, and on victory in October the military aircraft programme was soon targeted for filleting.

By April 1965, TSR.2, P.1154 and other military projects were history. However, to meet military requirements, American-built or American-designed and UK-equipped aircraft were bought instead. A full-scale retrenchment of British defence policy would come in 1967, largely impacting on some of these American purchases. However, the Wilson government still saw aerospace as a vital industry for commercial and strategic grounds and was prepared to fund a new generation of programmes but based on collaboration with Britain's European neighbours. Britain and France had already singed the Concorde Treaty and had begun talks on military collaboration. Although Labour also wanted to cancel the Concorde along with TSR.2, in 1965, the government-initiated talks leading to an Anglo-French military aircraft package and what would evolve into the European Airbus. Labour's collaborative strategy was underpinned by Lord Plowden's report into the state and future of the aerospace industry published in December 1965. This stated categorically that the United Kingdom would henceforward no longer develop large aircraft programmes independently, but seek international partners, primarily in Europe. Rolls-Royce, however, was explicitly excluded from this dictum and with the 1966 BSE take over was implicitly, if not explicitly, a 'national champion' of UK aerospace. The failure to press ahead with another Plowden recommendation to merge HSA and BAC left the aircraft side of the industry fragmented and less able to match the lobbying power of Rolls. This would have greater impact on the civil sector, but it would have an influence over key collaborative military programmes.

France

The governments of both the Fourth and Fifth French Republics (from 1958) adopted large-scale plans to shape post-war economic and industrial modernisation. Under General de Gaulle, the modernisation drive would assume overtly nationalistic overtones, embracing strategic independence from the United States and increasingly a vision of a French-led Europe. Aerospace would exemplify all these totems, industrial modernism, strategic independence (especially nuclear) and European technological competitiveness. The search for strategic autonomy would shape French military aerospace policy, with most combat designs developed domestically. Transport aircraft and civil airliner development was more open to international collaboration, but wherever possible under French leadership. This duality in French procurement policy enabled France to both maximise returns from defence sales abroad and the economic and technical benefits of collaboration. The French government was also sensitive to perceived gaps in domestic technological capability and sought either to fill these gaps or aggressively to protect indigenous resources. Unlike in the United Kingdom, leading companies were usually state-owned, although Dassault, primarily a military contractor, was a key exception, and indeed sometimes benefitted from offloading some of its overheads onto contracts with state-owned firms.

The presence of a clearly defined, consistent and long-term French strategy often impressed British observers. With some envy, the British trade association SBAC, this was 'one of the mechanisms to success that has already achieved results'.[9] On the other hand, French industrialists were sometimes critical of this 'top-down' approach, which undoubtedly took the commercial edge off many French actions. The annual budget might give consistency and certainty, but it was not always sufficient to support some key projects. The plan also delineated priorities, which were not always borne out by the market; the 6th plan in the 1970s placed Airbus third, behind the Concorde and the Mercure. From the 1970s, this rather mechanistic approach was replaced by a more flexible approach to aerospace planning.[10] However, aerospace was unequivocally viewed as a 'strategic industry' and as such the focus for intense political intervention. Thus, a 1977 French Parliamentary report noted, 'more than any other sphere of activity, aerospace is a test of strength

[9] SBAC Memorandum to House of Commons Select Committee on Science and Technology, HC.37, 1981–2.
[10] Cited in Keith Hayward, *International Collaboration in Civil Aerospace*, Frances Pinter, London 1986, pp. 38–9.

between states in which each participant deploys his technical and political forces'. The state, it followed, was 'an omnipresent actor' and a partner in industrial developments.[11]

Germany

Germany was effectively prohibited from aircraft manufacturing until NATO endorsed rearmament in the mid-1950s. From this point, the German government sought to establish the basis for a modern aerospace industry, in many cases based on the old pre-1945 companies. Much of the initial activity centred on licence production of American or British designs, followed in the late 1950s and early 1960s with collaborative work largely with the French on military transports. By the early 1960s, German industry, backed by national and regional governments, was looking to expand and take on more advanced work, again as a collaborative partner. A series of state-funded experimental military designs launched in the early 1960s served only to underline the unsustainable cost of sustaining an independent national programme. Germany had already joined France in developing the Transall military transport but was not immediately regarded either by Britain or France as a key partner in future advanced military programmes.

Until the mergers of the 1980s, German aerospace firms tended to be small compared even to their French and German counterparts. In some cases, family founders were still involved in corporate policymaking or had shares in the business. Several state and city governments invested in their local companies. The large German banks were also deeply involved as investors in aerospace through complex trust-based ownership structures. Up to the mid-1960s, most of German aerospace output was in the military sector, and the decision to join in the Airbus was driven by a deliberate decision to expand civil production. This was accompanied by government policies to increase the proportion of advanced military procurement sourced from domestic suppliers. Although well-funded, the German budgetary process could be protracted and its industrial and technical capabilities, though often first rate, were spread thinly. The German industry of the 1960s and 1970s was also predominantly an aircraft industry, with limited capabilities in aero-engines or equipment. Collaboration, however, was viewed as a means of strengthening national capabilities in both military and civil sectors.[12]

---

[11] Ibid, p. 38.
[12] Keith Hayward, *The West German Aerospace Industry and its Contribution to Western Security*, Whitehall Paper, Royal United Services Institute for Defence Studies, London 1990.

Early Anglo-French Collaborative Discussions

Initial efforts to forge intra-European military aerospace programmes were mainly under NATO auspices in the late 1950s. The so-called NMBR requirements were attempts to establish the basis for joint procurement and standardisation in NATO air forces. Although several did lead to production aircraft, few led to joint efforts. The Fiat G-91 light fighter helped to restart the Italian aerospace industry. The United Kingdom ignored the competition to focus on the Hawker Hunter; the British similarly turned down the Breguet Atlantique maritime patrol aircraft in favour of developing the Nimrod. The Atlantique was launched in the late 1950s as a collaborative programme involving France and Germany – the first effective example of a European collaborative programme. The Atlantique was followed by the Franco-German Transall military transport in 1959. Again, the United Kingdom decided on national solutions, including the Shorts Belfast, with decidedly mixed results. (The Belfast's performance was totally inadequate and built largely to protect employment in Northern Ireland.) The Transall faced fierce and ultimately overwhelming competition from the Lockheed C-130 Hercules, including sales to the United Kingdom following the 1965 cuts.

A British project, the P1127 Kestrel VSTOL was successful in a NATO competition in a run-off against a French design. But while the UK government and NATO funded a contract for two prototypes, later increased to four aircraft, the NATO-sponsored exercise ended in1961. While NATO lost interest, the UK government was prepared to fund further development. Narrowly escaping the 1965 round of budgetary cuts, as the Harrier, it went on to form the basis of the successful Anglo-American AV-8B programme of the early 1970s.[13] The British and French held some desultory discussions in the late 1950s about cooperation about military aerospace, but there was little common ground with cooperation stymied by powerful domestic industrial interests that favoured national pro-grammes. Relations had also been soured by the United Kingdom's 1956 rejec-tion of the French Caravelle airliner in favour of the Trident, despite the Caravelle's high British content.[14] Both countries were committed to their own national lines of development. The British had the TSR.2 and emerging concepts based on Hawker's VSTOL research programme. Dassault was already begin-ning to dominate French military aerospace and was acquiring a privileged access to the French MoD strengthened by personal links to President de Gaulle.[15] Both countries therefore had strong preferences for national programmes and without

---

[13] Keith Hayward, 'The One That Got Away', *Aviation Historian,* Issue 29, 2019, pp. 48–56.

[14] Including a de Haviland 'cockpit' and Rolls-Royce engines.

[15] Marcel Dassault had funded De Gaulle's political ambitions and was one of the richest men in France. His company was family owned, while much of the rest of French aerospace was owned by the state.

stronger economic reasons for compromising their independent military aerospace interests, collaboration would not be easy – and so it proved to be.

The breakthrough came with the supersonic transport (SST). Both the United Kingdom and France believed this to be the next logical step in civil aerospace development; but even based on the heroically pitched initial estimates of development costs, launching a viable commercial SST was unrealistic for either nation alone. The United Kingdom was at first inclined to work with the United States, but the latter's technical preferences and unwillingness to share development on an equal basis with the United Kingdom led inexorably to a cross-Channel link. In some respects, Concorde was not the ideal project to start the process of collaboration between the United Kingdom and France. It was, and arguably remains, the most complex and demanding design of post-war European aerospace. Indeed, one British civil servant described it as Europe's Apollo programme. Politically, however, it was possibly the only project that might have overcome the distrust borne of a decade of competition between the two national industries. Significantly, it was one of a kind in terms of political and industrial management, which was based on a two-page international treaty. Detailed management of the programme involving the four lead firms, BAC and Aerospatiale (airframe), BSE (Rolls-Royce from 1966) and Snecma (engine) had to be hammered out on an ad hoc basis, which ultimately required direct political intervention to establish a modus vivendi. This resulted in a reasonably effective management system, perhaps encouraged by the continual threat of cancellation that hung over Concorde from 1964.

The rapid escalation of development costs (later combined with a diminishing market) led the United Kingdom to threaten cancellation. This was thwarted on three occasions by French determination to proceed virtually at any cost. The United Kingdom was unable unilaterally to leave the project due to the Treaty obligations that had no provision to end development unless jointly agreed by the two governments. The United Kingdom was deterred from action by the threat of legal sanctions imposed following an International Court of Justice judgment. Politically, the British were also concerned not to damage the United Kingdom's prospects of joining the EEC with a protracted struggle with the French. Subsequent collaborative programmes would be based on less legally binding Memoranda of Understanding, with break points enabling governments to leave the programme; initial negotiations setting up programmes would also establish criteria for project management and government supervision. Nevertheless, despite these changes more sophisticated structures would not diminish the politics associated with collaborative programmes. Indeed, with more points at which a participant could leave a programme, crises would become more frequent, generally increasing the uncertainties associated with collaborative projects.

These tensions were for the future; in the short term, the Concorde Treaty and the relatively successful merging of two national industries in a common effort rekindled the idea of cooperation on military programmes. The two countries began talks about future collaborative options in the early 1960s under the auspices of the Anglo-French Aircraft Working Group. A NATO-wide require-ment for a VSTOL fighter seemed a good opportunity to move matters forward towards a substantive project. The logic of working together was clear from a November 1962 letter from the British Minister of Defence Julian Amery to his French opposite number, Pierre Messmer. It was 'unfortunate', Amery wrote, '[t]hat both countries are spending large sums of money on different approaches to the problem of a VTOL strike fighter'. He concluded:

> I do not underestimate the difficulty of reaching agreement on reciprocal or joint projects of the kind we have discussed. The political and economic obstacles may well prove formidable. At the same time, I do not see how countries like ours will long be able to maintain the military strength, which their political responsibility requires unless we can share some of the work together. France and Britain seem to be well on the way to a large-scale joint enterprise on the civil side with the supersonic airliner. It would indeed be a great thing if we could match this achievement with some similar joint endeavour in the sphere of defence.[16]

To this, Messmer replied positively, if non-committal on specifics, 'In November there had been a perfect atmosphere of understanding. I attach just as much importance to examining the possibilities of agreement on the defin-ition of military requirements and operational characteristics.'[17]

The British felt that they had the stronger opening position: the HSA P.1154 ducted fan concept was the most sophisticated approach to the specification and earlier NATO interest in the Kestrel confirmed their opinion that this was the best way to go forward. The French preferred a simpler design using separate lift engine approach adopted by the Dassault-Sud Aviation Balzac, essentially a Mirage III with Rolls-Royce and BSE engines. The French were quick to point to this latter feature underlining the Balzac's established Anglo-French creden-tials. Following another NATO technical assessment in May 1962, the P.1154 was declared the better design on technical grounds – its ducted thrust concept was far superior to the multi-engined approach of the Mirage III-V, but the latter was felt to offer more industrial work share opportunities. As a result, the two

---

[16] Letter from Minister of Defence Julian Amery to French Minister of Defence Pierre Messmer, 27th November 1962, UK National Archive Kew (NA) Air 2/16735.

[17] Reply from Messmer, 27th November 1962, NA Air 2/16735.

aircrafts were declared joint winners, a decision hardly conducive to making progress towards a substantive multinational project.

Thorneycroft and the British MoD began to conceive of an alternative strategy: in order to satisfy national industrial interests as well as delivering aircraft (and missiles) suited to both nations' armed services, it might be better to think in terms of a 'package' of programmes. In a note to the Cabinet, Thorneycroft argued that if the French were to take P.1154, 'It would be plainly necessary for the British side to take something of considerable importance from France.' In this respect a high-speed helicopter project under development in France would seem to fit. A similar bargain would follow if French could be induced to take an interest in the TSR.2 – a somewhat optimistic view given that the Dassault IV nuclear bomber was about to enter service. If so, the United Kingdom would have to consider similar level of commitment, which could be to take a French aircraft to meet the UK requirement of a new maritime reconnaissance aircraft. The two sides were also looking at aspects of military space, including communications satellites and a manned spacecraft; but this would be 'as far away as middle of next decade'.[18]

The formation of several other specialist working groups, including helicopters, high-speed low-level aircraft weapon systems and guided weapons, helped to move things along. There were a series of industrial visits, including a French inspection of the TSR.2 facilities and a full briefing from BAC. However, while many papers were exchanged, there was very little progress reported towards common requirements. Indeed, British officials suggested suspension of formal contacts until both sides had more fully studied the issues.[19] Nevertheless, Julian Amery was sufficiently confident that the two countries could still collaborate on the P.1154, 'We have little doubt that ours is the better horse and there are unconfirmed rumours that the Mirage 3 is running onto difficulties. M. Messmer feels, as I do, that if the British and French can agree quickly on a VTOL ground attack aircraft, we should be able to corner the whole European market.' Amery was also optimistic that they could trade-off French participation in the TSR.2 for the Shackleton replacement. He also felt that he could leverage French unhappiness with the Germans over potential helicopter developments.[20]

In the event, Amery's optimism was somewhat premature. The British side felt that the ducted airflow approach was far superior to France's commitment to the separate lift engine, 'We have little doubt that ours is the better horse.'[21]

---

[18] Note to Cabinet, 27th November 1962, NA Air 2/16735.

[19] Anglo-French Aircraft Working Group, NA Air 2/16735.

[20] Memorandum to Cabinet from Minister of Defence Julian Amery, 18th January 1963, NA Air 2/ 16735.

[21] Memorandum from Minister of Defence Julian Amery, 18th January 1963, NA PREM 11/ 4092.

However, the February meeting of the working group revealed divergence over key requirements; the French were fundamentally opposed to the vectored thrust approach to VSTOL and there were considerable differences between the two countries over range and timescales. Indeed, the French clearly preferred a version of the Dassault Mirage 3 with its proven supersonic capability, although its ability to transition to supersonic speed after a vertical take-off was questionable. By the end of February, British officials felt that the opportunity to seal a collaborative deal was slipping away – a position not helped by the fact that the United Kingdom itself had still to commit money to the P.1154: 'If we can get a decision on the P.1154 before the next meeting we will clearly be in a stronger position, even this would not I believes be enough to get them to change their minds at this juncture.'[22]

Even as hopes of a comprehensive joint programme began to fade, Peter Thorneycroft, who replaced Amery as Minister of Defence in February 1963, noted, 'It would be a great pity to let the impetus fade. It would be unfortunate both from the point of view of the British aircraft industry and against the background that we must all hope for an improvement in Anglo-French political relations in due course.' The importance of maintaining links with the French were even more important politically after the breakdown in the EEC talks; 'we should continue to co-operate in all fields where it is of practical advantage for us do so. This clearly applies to the kind of research and development projects discussed in the draft letter'. It was agreed that links would be maintained at a ministerial level in the hope that substantive progress might yet be made. However, there was little substantive progress before the 1964 general election.[23]

The fundamental problem with these talks was that both sides had their own already well-formulated projects on offer. The TSR.2 was always likely to be a hard sell given that the programme was so far into development and could hardly offer the French much in the way of work share. There were fundamental differences over the VSTOL options and even if the British were convinced that the vectored thrust approach was technically superior, 'the French are not going to admit a possibility of abandoning their project, believing that each state had made its choice solely for political and industrial reasons'. The British were not very keen on the Atlantique to replace the Shackleton, believing the French design to be technically inadequate. On the other hand, there was still some hope that something might be achieved in the helicopter and guided weapons fields.[24]

---

[22] Minutes of Meeting in Paris of Anglo-French Aircraft Working Group 26 – 7th February 1963; UK briefing 20th February 1963, NA Air 2/1673.

[23] Peter Thorneycroft memorandum to Prime Minister, 4th February 1963, NA PREM 11/ 4092.

[24] Air Ministry commentary on Anglo-French Aircraft Working Group meeting, 26th April 1963, NA Air 2/16735.

However, while many of these military contacts tended to drift into the sand, the discussions about future programmes without the baggage of mature or near-mature commitments would in time be fruitful; the 1964 agreement to develop the air-to-ground Martel missile based on joint work between Hawker Siddeley and the French firm Matra was something of a breakthrough. Work sharing was based on a common core such as the motor and airframe, with two weapons – an HSA TV-guided missile and Matra's anti-radar system.[25] A wider-ranging agreement on Anglo-French military projects would come after the October 1964 general election. Not all of these would reach production, and in time Britain's' primary partner in military aircraft would be Germany, not France, but as in the civil sector, the future of UK aerospace would hencefor-ward be primarily as a partner in European enterprises.

The 1965 Anglo-French Military Aircraft Package

Earlier Anglo-French negotiations had been clouded by the existence of com-peting national projects, but most of these at least on the British disappeared with the 1965 cull of UK domestic projects. Between 1964 and 1966, the Labour government renewed talks with the French covering helicopters, guided weapons and combat aircraft.[26] The UK Treasury was worried that it might be railroaded into expensive commitments largely to satisfy political interests:

'We ought to consider very carefully indeed whether the British aircraft industry is in fact capable of taking on another ultra-sophisticated job ... this is clearly one that has considerable political overtones: this hardly seems a well-chosen moment to decide it. It would be the height of folly to build aircraft for which there is no immediate need, and the proposal that this is put as a "preliminary study" does not wash.'[27]

However, working together, the Ministry of Aviation (MoA, shortly to be absorbed into the Ministry of Technology, Mintech) and the MoD outman-oeuvred the Treasury, and in February 1965, the two governments agreed a draft Memorandum of Understanding (MoU) on a strike/trainer aircraft, work on guided weapons and helicopters, and a further commitment to study a more advanced interceptor/strike aircraft with variable geometry wings – the AFVG.[28] The helicopter deal was a case of each side undertaking to buy an

---

[25] NA CAB 129/118/68, 8th September 1964, pp.

[26] Treasury Memorandum, 2nd October 1964, NA T225/2771; For a detailed study of the AFVG see Keith Hayward, 'The AFVG'. *The Aviation Historian,* Issue 31, 2021, pp. 64–70.

[27] Treasury Memorandum, 20th January 1965, NA T225/2771; Treasury Memorandum, 2nd October 1964, NA T225/2771.

[28] Anglo-French draft Memorandum of Understanding to study fixed and VG wing options February 1965, NA T225/2771.

aircraft largely developed by the other: the British taking the Puma and Gazelle in return for French procurement of the Lynx. The missile package was a more sophisticated co-development of a common airframe equipped to meet different national requirements. The British government greeted the package with some gusto: Minister of Defence Denis Healey described Franco-British cooperation as the 'logic of things', while Aviation Minister Roy Jenkins stated that the package was the 'essential foundation for the future of the British aircraft industry'.[29]

From the outset, there were differences between the two sides over timing and specifications of both fighter aircrafts. In the event, the training requirement was dropped from the collaborative package, each side going on to develop its own trainer aircraft.[30] The 'strike-trainer' would thus turn into the basis for the Jaguar fighter.[31] The 1965 package deal awarded 'design leadership' for the Jaguar to the French company Breguet with BAC in a 'junior' position, although given the relative lack of experience on the part of Breguet BAC Warton would play a more significant role in development. Breguet had the full support of the French government because it was one of the weaker elements in the French aircraft industry and at this stage the French government was keen to maintain some competition with Dassault. But with the loss of a large chunk of its advanced military business ending with the TSR.2, BAC was in a weak position to argue about leadership. To balance French leadership of the airframe, Rolls-Royce would lead a joint engine programme with Turbomeca, which up to this point had only produced turbo-shaft engines for helicopters. There was little doubt here as to which company was the junior partner; this partnership would produce the highly successful Adour engine.[32]

The French were also keen at this stage to keep the talks on a bilateral basis; the Germans had shown some interest in the VG concept (they had also been working on a VSTOL design), but the French Minister of Aviation told Aviation Minister Jenkins that they 'should not be in too much of a hurry to bring the Germans into association with the projects covered by the (Anglo-French) agreement'. 'Progress', he said, 'could only suffer if too many people were brought into them'. He was also concerned that collaboration with Germany would only create another competitor to both countries – 'a serious rival'. Jenkins accepted this as far as the R&D phase was concerned, but he felt that the German market was too important to be left out of the equation for future

---

[29] Keith Hayward, *The British Aircraft Industry*, Manchester University Press, Manchester, 1989, p. 109.

[30] These would be the Franco-German Alpha Jet and the Hawk.

[31] Hayward, *The British Aircraft Industry*, p. 109.

[32] The Adour would also power the Hawk strike trainer in the 1970s.

consideration. He was also concerned to avoid any 'danger of either France or Britain being tempted to play off the Germans against the other'.[33] Indeed, the interplay between the three countries would become a persistent feature of European aerospace cooperation over the next sixty years.

BAC's partnership with Breguet worked well from the outset as both badly needed the business and had every incentive to pool their efforts in a smooth and efficient manner. The Breguet team of Henri Zeigler (later a key figure in the Concorde and Airbus programmes) and his senior staff 'welcomed collaboration and genuinely tried to make it work on an equal partnership basis'. Ivan Yates, Warton's project leader and his French colleague Jean Beron 'worked well together and the project proceeded rapidly'. BAC with Sir George Edwards' experience of the Concorde's cumbersome international management processes in mind was keen to establish a clearly defined international centralised structure. This was delivered by SEPECAT, a French-registered holding company with BAC and Breguet acting as subcontractors to the jointly owned prime contractor. The relationship would become more fraught with the merger of Dassault and Breguet with claims from the British side that Dassault preferred to promote sales of its own aircraft when they competed with the Jaguar. However, these later tensions were nothing compared to those generated by the AFVG.[34]

Politically, the two sides had very different views about the importance that should be assigned to the AFVG. To the British government, it was a vital programme and was presented as the 'core of our long-term aircraft programme destined to provide the main strike element for the RAF'.[35] However, the French requirement for a new pure strike aircraft was less urgent, and which would in the medium terms be satisfied by continued developments of the Dassault Mirage family. As discussions moved on, French industrial interests increasingly shaped development. BAC would be partnered by Avions Marcel Dassault, still owned and controlled by its founder and his family. Marcel Dassault for his part believed that his company 'was capable of building a variable geometry aircraft on its own and did not need the British' – as a British official later noted, his 'successes and wealth have made him a law unto himself'.[36]

---

[33] Notes of meeting between French and British aviation ministers, 19th June 1965, NA AVIA63/123.

[34] Hayward, *The British Aircraft Industry,* p. 109.

[35] Letter to Pierre Messmer from Denis Healey, 15th February 1966, NA T225/2650; Hayward, *The British Aircraft Industry,* pp. 111.

[36] Claude Carlier, *Marcel Dassault, la legend d'un siècle*, Paris 1992, p. 24; Memorandum to Prime Minister Harold Wilson from Sir Solly Zukerman 9th June 1967, NA CAB 164/351.

Dassault certainly had the support of the French procurement agency, DMA. Industry and government had a common interest in maximising sales of Dassault military aircraft. This entailed quietly promoting an indigenous alternative, the Mirage 3 G, to the collaborative programme during the protracted AFVG negotiations. The French claimed that this was an 'insurance' against UK withdrawal and to fill a gap in Dassault's design office work. The French, it was stated, 'understood our concern at the likely effect on the BAC-Dassault relationship. But they state they have no intention of running a single-engined VG against the twin specified in the MoU'. The MoA hoped to see the French drop the Mirage 3 G, possibly aided by a proposal to develop a research vehicle in support of the AFVG, which would help Dassault's loading problem, but not necessarily satisfy the French insurance interest.[37]

From the outset, the British was concerned about the possibility that the French might opt for the Mirage 3 G and that Dassault's heavy lobbying would carry the French government; as BAC's Sir George Edwards put it, 'It is hard to believe that Dassault, with their political power and their eye to the main chance, will not exploit and sell this aircraft if they get any chance of doing so profitably', a view echoed by the MoA, 'This is essentially a political problem for both sides.'[38] If the relationship between Dassault and BAC was difficult, Rolls-Royce, left out of the AFVG programme in favour of BSE, believed that the BSE/Snecma M-45 engine would open the door to the Americans via licence agreements with P&W. In 1966, Rolls moved to counter the M-45 with its own RB.153, claiming it to be superior technically and cheaper to develop, an option that had support from the MoD, as one senior official wrote to his MoA opposite number, 'I hope you will be able to agree that we can make it a primary objective to go for the RB.153.'[39]

The perceived technical advantages of a change in engine choice notwithstanding, the Treasury was alert to the industrial and political implications, domestically and internationally: 'It remains to be seen whether a change is practicable in terms of domestic politics and relations with the French'; and dropping the M.45 would effectively put BSE out of the advanced military engine business. Moreover, the M.45 was the first major engine programme

---

[37] Marc R. de Vore and Moritz Weiss, 'Who's in the cockpit? The political economy of collaborative aircraft decisions', *Review of International Political Economy*, 21:2, pp. 512–14. Quietly, but not secretly, as some British observers have asserted see, Ministry of Aviation note, *French VG Research Aircraft*, 10th November 1965; NA AVIA 65/1799.

[38] Memorandum, re letter from Sir George Edwards, 23rd February 1966; Ministry of Aviation Memorandum, 15th April 1966; NA AVIA 65/1799.

[39] Ministry of Defence letter to Sir Richard Way, Permanent Secretary, Ministry of Aviation. 15th March 1966, NA T225/2650.

developed wholly in France (other programmes had been helped by links with P&W).[40]

The MoA threw its support for the Rolls engine. With Snecma/BSE working on the Olympus for the Concorde and a strong contender for the European 'airbus', Rolls would be left dangerously exposed:

> This leaves virtually nothing for Rolls in the big engine field in the 1970s, with European leadership in the engine field being shared with the French who will have built themselves up on UK technology and with UK financial assistance. This situation adds good commercial and political reasons for not choosing the M.45 and adopting the Rolls engine. A large part of the extra cost of the M.45 can be attributed to the French efforts to build up their aero industry, and in this context, it can be pointed out to the French that this is no part of our agreement with them, especially at cost to ourselves.[41]

The MoD/MoA alliance pressed hard to switch to the RB.153, but it was hard to see how Snecma could retain 'design leadership' of a Rolls engine. Indeed, Healey was advised that it might be better to allow Dassault to lead the aircraft in compensation, a view that BAC was hardly ready swallow.

Deliberations through the spring and summer of 1966 proved inconclusive, with the British keener to move forward than the French, who refused to budge on the engine question. The British were inclined to maintain a hard line as European collaboration depended on a full partnership in all aspects of industry and could not depend upon 'outside forces'. In the event, Rolls moved unilaterally to head off the threat from P&W; in June 1966, Rolls-Royce acquired BSE and allowed the P&W licence to lapse – *fautes de mieux* Seneca had to partner with Rolls.[42] However, the AFVG was already looking precarious as the French began to raise budgetary reasons for preferring a cheaper national alternative 'something on the lines of the Mirage 3 G. French and British thinking on VG may be becoming incompatible'.[43] The two sides were now beginning to divide sharply over specifications and timing, reflecting (or caused by) the differences over engine selection.[44]

If the engine choice had dominated negotiations, the British government had also woken up to the implications for BAC should the AFVG collapse. In October 1966, Denis Healey was prepared to endorse a request from the MoA

---

[40] Ibid.

[41] Briefing for Healey meeting with Messmer on AFVG, 6th May 1966 and Ministry of Aviation appendix on engine choice, NA T225/2650.

[42] Record of meeting between French and British Ministers of Defence, 6th May 1966, NA T225/2650; Denis Healey Memorandum to PM 13th May 1966, NA T225/2651; Anglo-French aircraft projects meeting briefing paper, July 1966, NA T225/2651.

[43] Record of meeting between French and British Ministers of Defence, 27th July 1966: Foreign Office Note of meeting between PM and President de Gaulle, 8th July 1966; NA T225/2651; MoD/MoA memorandum, 7th October 1966, NA T225/2651.

[44] MoD/MoA memorandum, 7th October 1966, NA T225/2651.

to support 'our own version' of a VG aircraft if the French abandoned the project. The future of BAC Warton was of paramount importance; it was essential to protect BAC's supersonic experience and the research facilities on the Warton site; 'our conclusion therefore is that the future military project decisions should be directed towards concentrating combat aircraft design on the BAC team at Warton, and that to preserve the nucleus of the present team it is essential to embark forthwith on a VG aircraft or its equivalent'.[45] At a working level, the Dassault and BAC Warton engineers got on 'extremely well together and could have formed a superb joint team to lead the world in military aviation but Dassault pride and ambition would not permit it'. From their perspective, the idea that BAC could lead the programme was 'an idea counter to nature'. Despite BAC's nominal leadership of the AFVG, Dassault insisted on taking the technical lead. As Sir George Edwards observed, 'Marcel Dassault was never going to accept (BAC leadership). Considering the power he held in France, I read the eventual doom of the AFVG in one conversation.'[46]

Despite hints that all was not well with the pace and direction of negotiations, the British government continued to argue that the Anglo-French package, including the AFVG, was an 'essential foundation for the future of the British aircraft industry'. Minister of Defence Healey told the House of Commons in February 1967 that 'without this project there would be no design work for the British aircraft industry not only in Britain but in Europe. That is the sense in which this is the core of our long-term aircraft programme'. But by April 1967, matters reached a critical point; a meeting between French and British officials on the 7 April was described as 'pretty disastrous'. Dassault was accused of being 'completely unwilling to cooperate with BAC' and had placed 'obstacles in the way of a joint effort'. Dassault's lobbying was paying off and had secured both support for the Mirage 3 G, officially unveiled at the Paris airshow in June, and its takeover of Breguet, BAC's partner on the Jaguar.[47]

On 29 June, the French announced their withdrawal from the AFVG. BAC believed that the French had stalled on the AFVG until the Mirage 3 G was sufficiently advanced to present 'a *fait accompli* that the British would have been pressed to buy from France; meanwhile they had got us firmly locked into the

---

[45] *The Future of the Airframe Industry*, Memorandum to the Cabinet, 18th October 1966, NA CAB 129/127/1; Memorandum from Defence Secretary, 1st December 1966, NA DEFE 13/551.

[46] Robert Gardner, *From Bouncing Bombs to Concorde: The Biography of Sir George Edwards,* The History Press: London, 2006, p. 137; Jean Cabriere, a long-term colleague of Marcel Dassault cited in Charles Carlier, *Marcel Dassault, la legende d'un siecle*, Paris, 1992, p. 241.

[47] Treasury Memorandum 3rd April 1967; Minutes of Anglo-French Joint Defence Projects Board, 7th April 1967; Memorandum from Denis Healey to PM, 12th April 1967; NA T225/2858; Treasury Memorandum 3rd April 1967; Minutes of Anglo-French Joint Defence Projects Board, 7th April 1967; Memorandum from Denis Healey to PM, 12th April 1967; NA T225/2858; Hayward, *The British Aircraft Industry*, p. 109 and p. 111.

(Jaguar) programme under French leadership'. Unknown even to BAC, Dassault was also working on a more conventional concept, the F1, which would eventually meet the French Air Force requirement. However, when BAC eventually got wind of this, British officials again 'seemed to have no knowledge of it'.[48] The collapse of the AFVG was deeply embarrassing to the government, who were accused of having put all its aircraft 'eggs in the collaborative basket'. Labour had now spent over £250 million on abortive military programmes, much the same amount as the maligned Conservative government in the early 1960s. The government, and Healey personally, were thoroughly discomforted by the AFVG affair. It only confirmed the view of Sir George Edwards and others that the United Kingdom had to be able to lead international ventures or to develop national programmes where the collaborative option was inadequate or questionable.[49] The Mirage F1 continued the Dassault family of relatively cheap and exportable national products; the British aerospace industry, on the other hand, would have to find another set of international partners.

Multilateral Cooperation – the MRCA/Tornado

Following the collapse of the AVFG, Sir Burke Trend, the Cabinet Secretary, was despondent, 'There is no route on our own, but who is the best partner? USA is too big for comfort, France too chauvinist for reliability. Germany? Italy, Holland (too small). I conclude, until we go in the EEC, we should cooperate where we can, putting Germany first.'[50] At an industrial level, the government continued to support BAC's work on variable geometry while Denis Healey tried to assemble another international coalition to fill the gap in both BAC's workload and RAF requirements. Without a new project,

> [w]e must face the fact that the BAC team at Warton will melt away almost immediately. This will remove our capacity to develop airframes for advanced military aircraft. In time, this would call into question of how long we would remain able to develop independently comparable military engines. We should in fact be faced with a virtual disappearance of the military side of the aircraft industry, with inevitable repercussions on the civil side. This would mean a rapid decline in the industry as a whole with all the consequent effects on technology and employment.[51]

---

[48] Report of Meeting between PM and French President 19th June 1967; NA T225/2944; DeVore & Weiss, Who's in the cockpit? The political economy of collaborative aircraft decisions, p. 513; Keith Hayward, *Freddie Gage; Aerospace Engineer and Businessman; The life and times of Sir Frederick Page, CBE, MA, FEng, Hon. FRAeS*, RAeS, RAeS Paper, 2013.

[49] Hayward, *The British Aircraft Industry*, p. 111.

[50] Handwritten note, 28th September 1967, NA CAB 164/351.

[51] Memorandum by Secretary of State for Defence and Secretary of State for Technology, 29th June 1967; NA T225/2944.

The main contender for Healey's 'gap filler' was the Multirole Combat Aircraft (MRCA) – an F-104 replacement needed by several NATO powers, including Germany, a market for over 1,500 sales. The Germans were also looking to build up their aerospace industry, and working with the British was an attractive prospect. While other possible partners dropped out of contention early in the process, la quartet of nations – Britain, Germany, Italy and Holland – remained interested in the MRCA. In London, the absence of realistic alternatives was adding to the pressure to seal a deal with the Germans, even though Bonn's industrial ambitions seemed at odds with the German capabilities.[52]

There were good military reasons for developing the MRCA – it was consistent with new NATO strategic doctrine of Flexible Response, which had replaced the Massive (nuclear) Retaliation doctrine in 1968 and emphasised the role of conventional forces.[53] Equally, given the recent AFVG debacle, Healey was under domestic political pressure to salvage something for the UK combat aircraft industry. To the Treasury, however, the prospect of the MRCA was 'clearly still in a fearful muddle. MoD ministers still need to be convinced of the need for this aircraft and validity of the UK requirement, which is more complex and costly than the Europeans'. Treasury officials feared a repeat of the AFVG debacle: 'Such a result would effectively dish European collaboration for a long period and would, given the past history on aircraft projects, haunt the Labour Government and the Defence Secretary personally.' Officials warned that too much 'public effervescence' about relations with Germany on Healey's part could cloud judgement about the debate over requirements and industrial arrangements.[54] Italy and Spain also declared an interest in the MRCA, although early Dutch and Canadian participation in the talks soon faded.

Initially, sorting out the industrial arrangements looked as fraught as working with the French. Although both BAC and Rolls were far superior and more experienced that their German opposite numbers, the Germans 'want to lead on the project centring it on Munich. This poses interesting questions about the continuing viability of the Warton design team and whole question of whether we need to retain an advanced military design capability with its (questionable) fall-out effects on the civil aircraft industry'.[55] There was strong German political pressure to 'get into advanced technology', but Healey promised fully to share technology and design responsibilities with the Germans. But

---

[52] Keith Hayward, 'Out of the Ashes – MRCA and the birth of the Tornado', *The Aviation Historian*, Issue No. 37, November 2021, pp. 10–18.

[53] A rationale that also saved the Harrier, see Hayward, 'The One That Got Away'.

[54] Treasury memorandum, 15th October 1968, NA T 225/3187; Note of meeting between MoD official and Treasury, 17th October 1968, NA T 225/3187.

[55] Treasury memorandum, 15th October 1968, NA T 225/3187; Note of meeting between MoD official and Treasury, 17th October 1968, NA T 225/3187.

given BAC's dependence on a successful outcome, as well as saving Healey's face, the British position was somewhat precarious.[56]

German determination to 'lead' the programme rested on several points; the ostensible German order was larger than Britain's; the Luftwaffe planned to receive the aircraft first and the design leadership would help to mitigate their risk; and the size of the respective companies should have no bearing on the allocation of technical responsibilities.[57] From the British perspective, especially on the part of the Warton contingent, this was an unacceptable set of demands. The crux of the matter was to find a way of satisfying German demands without compromising the programme, which effectively meant ensuring a powerful position for Warton. The problem was exacerbated by the likelihood that the accompanying engine programme would be dominated by Rolls-Royce, which if used to balance commitments on the aircraft could seriously erode BAC's eventual work share to the point that it would be 'nonviable'. However, the British government saw Rolls' place as a defining aspect of the programme and was non-negotiable.[58] In the event, the question of 'industrial leadership' was finessed by the creation of two transnational management organisations, Panavia and Turbo Union, both registered in Munich.

Two industrial issues remained a source of tension. Again, Rolls' position was, as we have noted, non-negotiable. The Germans suggested that an American engine might be used instead, which led immediately to a de facto veto from the British. In the United Kingdom, Mintech made it clear that the RB.199 was 'their main interest in the MRCA'.[59] The Treasury was again pessimistic about reaching a final agreement: 'The MRCA smells of the graveyard', and he believed that neither MoD nor Mintech was 'particularly enthusiastic', and the latter would 'much prefer a national project'. But there was a 'tremendous political head of steam' as MRCA was the only non-US aircraft in sight capable of measuring up to the 'customarily exacting requirements of the air staff'. There was an ominous and recent comparison:

> As we see it, the MRCA falls into the category of projects, of which the TSR.2 is the most obvious, but by no means the only example which tries to advance technology on too many fronts. A national programme could be studied longer with no commitment, but the collaborative context implies we could soon be too deeply committed to withdraw.

---

[56] Note of discussion between Denis Healey and Dr. G Shroder, 9th–11th October 1968, NA T 225/3187 and note of talk with German Foreign Secretary von Dohnani, Treasury official comment, 21st October 1968, NA T225/3187.

[57] Anonymous German industrialist, *Flight International*, 31st October 1968.

[58] Air Ministry note to FCO, 22nd October 1968, NA T 225/3187; Treasury note, 13th November 1968, NA T 225/3187.

[59] Treasury note, 30th January 1969, NA T225/3189; Treasury note 1st April 1969, NA T225/3191.

In the event, the American challenge to Rolls-Royce disappeared, particularly as it became evident that a collaborative development programme with the British would benefit the German aero-engine sector considerably more than any licence-build production based on an American design.[60] This cleared the way for a two-year £7 million project definition phase signed in May 1969.

The second major industrial divergence came later in the programme. While the Germans were evidently inferior in many respects to BAC and MBB, their electronics industry was strongly placed. However, the German position on advanced avionics was not so well developed. The German claim was underpinned by the need to distribute work fairly both quantitatively and qualitatively. In order to fulfil German work-sharing entitlements, its less experienced avionics industry wanted to use American licenced technologies, pre-eminently an attack radar to be based on the Texas Instruments system developed for the F-111 as the basis for a German-led radar programme. Using American technology would also save money – a UK-designed alternative was estimated to cost £40 million more. However, while the British felt that a European project should not depend on American technology, the German solution was accepted primarily on political grounds.[61]

There was also a final political irritation: in 1972, the Germans cut their order from 600 to 324, raising the suspicion that they had inflated their initial order to win a larger share of the development and production. BAC's Freddie Page had no doubts on this score:

> The Germans overbid their proposed order to secure industrial advantage for Germany and the British rather underbid knowing that they would later wish to introduce a requirement for an Air Defence Variant, ADV. After some time, too late to be practicable to alter the industrial balance significantly, the Germans reduced their order; the British increased theirs by introducing the ADV and, to everybody's surprise, the Italians remained completely firm in their order for 100 aircraft.[62]

However, in September 1971, the MRCA was confirmed and named Tornado. This confirmed the presence of a least two European centres of combat aircraft development – the multilateral Panavia team and the national French grouping led by Dassault.

---

[60] Treasury note 2nd April 1969, NA T225/3191 Cabinet minute, 4th September 1969, NA CAB/128/44/42; Cabinet minute, 8th May 1969, NA CAB/128/44/22.

[61] Cited in Keith Hayward, *The British Aircraft Industry*, p. 114. The Ferranti ADV radar was notoriously late and over cost – caustically called the 'Blue Circle' radar after the concrete used to fill the aircraft's nose as a temporary measure. Brief for the prime minister (Edward Heath), 22nd June and 28th July 1971, NA PREM 15/1374.

[62] Hayward, *Freddie Page*.

Eurofighter 1985–90 – France Stays Aloof

In the late 1970s, along with other European and American companies, the United Kingdom began to consider another generation of fighter aircraft. The United Kingdom and France both launched demonstrator aircraft to prove advanced aerodynamic and control technologies. In 1984, this work converged to consider development of a European Combat Aircraft (ECA), later designated the EFA. Discussions linked the 'Panavia' Group, Britain, Germany and Italy with France (and Spain) in a joint five-nation programme. Despite two years of intense official and industrial activity, the five-nation EFA had become the four-nation Eurofighter/Typhoon, with France going it alone with the Dassault Rafale. The failure to launch a five-nation programme was the result of irreconcilable industrial and military differences again caused largely by Anglo-French conflicts of interest. The result was to reaffirm a schism in ECA development that would last into the early twenty-first century.

By the late 1970s, both France and the United Kingdom were looking for successors to their respective main combat aircraft, the Tornado and the Mirage 2000. The newly rationalised and nationalised British Aerospace (BAe) cofounded the £150 million Experimental Aircraft Programme (EPA) with the MoD. Over 40 per cent of the industry contribution came from the equipment sector, led by GEC Avionics, Smiths and Ferranti, and complemented by an engine demonstrator, the Rolls-Royce XG40. The EAP was also funded in part by some of the Panavia partners, but the German government was reluctant to close off the possibility of working with France. The French also supported a Dassault demonstrator, the ACX, and a new Snecma engine, the M.88.[63] Of the two, France was the more likely to continue its largely independent path in combat aircraft development than the United Kingdom. Indeed, defence budgetary cuts in the early and mid-1970s had ended immediate hopes that the RAF would look for a Phantom replacement. This left the newly nationalised BAe with a hiatus in its military aircraft programme. The Harrier 11, with a more powerful Pegasus engine, was initially abandoned, but in the mid-1970s development was subsumed into an American-led project which became the AV-8B. However, this left BAe Warton with little work other than Tornado upgrades. There were tentative attempts to build another European consortium, but these had faded by 1981, and the 1981 defence review confirmed there would be 'no immediate replacement for the Jaguar'.[64]

---

[63] Ivan Yates, *Evolution of the New European Fighter*, BAe, 1988, pp. 28–35. For a details of the EAP, see Alan Seabridge and Leon Skorczewski, *EAP*, BAe, 2016.

[64] *A Future Fighter Aircraft for the RAF; Consideration of the Options*, Paper by Ministry of Defence Equipment Policy Committee, 2nd April 1985, NA DEFE72/411.

BAe's response was the private venture P110 aiming at a draft RAF requirement for an agile multirole fighter. To save money and time on development, the
P110 would use Tornado systems, including a version of the RB.199 engine. It
was conceived as a direct competitor to the Dassault Mirage 2000, aiming at the
lucrative Middle East market. BAe needed a production run of 500 to launch the
programme but believed it would generate £4,500 million in sales. The project
would be funded by a consortium of Arab states, but still depended on some
backing from the British government. BAe and its development partners would
carry early development costs, minimising 'MoD spend in early years', effectively 'lending money to the MoD who eventually pay back on indexed terms'.
Failure to launch the aircraft would seriously harm BAe's future as a major
combat aircraft producer, leaving France as the dominant player in the European
aerospace scene. The Treasury, however, saw this as a blatant way of evading
the constraints on defence spending.[65]

A Treasury analysis finally concluded that BAe's case that the P110 could be
justified on 'national security grounds': Without the P110

> BAe will forfeit its design capability in the field of conventional combat
> aircraft. Any further needs of such aircraft for the RAF will have to be
> supplied from foreign sources, probably from the US or France. Apart from
> the defence strategy implications of relying on an overseas supplier with the
> risk of disruption in the flow of supplies for political reasons, there are also
> industrial policy aspects.[66]

Other Treasury officials were less enthusiastic: one official noted, 'I am worried
by the prominence given to P110. Everyone is in danger of being hypnotised by
BAe and Rolls-Royce propaganda. My understanding is that the P110 was
dreamed up for the Arabs as a substitute for the Tornado whose sale the
Germans are blocking.'[67]

In September 1981, BAe's Sir Austin Pearce wrote to the prime minister,
pressing the case for the P110 and other possible sales in the Middle East. He
noted that despite support from the MoD defence Sales team, the French threat
was as strong as ever. Jordan had shown some interest in the P110 and Tornado,
but 'had no money'. In sales tours of the region the MoD sought to sidestep the
lack of RAF interest in the P110 by referring to the 'family' of technology it
represented, which was supported by the United Kingdom 'on the technical

---

[65] Paper by BAe, *P110 Launching*, January 1982, NA FCO46/3238; DTI Memorandum 4th
August 1981, NA FV17/432; for the full story of the Iraqi deal see Keith Hayward, 'Selling to
Sadham; Iraq and the P110/Tornado package, 1981–2", *Aviation Historian*, Issue 42,
January 2023.
[66] Treasury Memorandum, *British Aerospace and the UK Economy*, 22nd April 1982, NA T457/6.
[67] Treasury Note, 26th April 1982, NA T457/6.

side'. More positively, although the German government was reluctant to allow Tornado sales to the Middle East as a 'zone of conflict', the British government felt that a new MoU on sales of collaborative projects would remove a total German veto. Other potential customers included Iraq, but the Foreign Secretary Lord Carrington was dubious – 'Tornado in Iraqi hands was disagreeable.'[68]

Two crucial events intervened finally to kill the deal with Iraq, and to avoid a more than embarrassing contest between Iraqi and RAF Tornados in 1991: the first of these was a more lucrative contract with Saudi Arabia, the Al Yamamah contract which included the same Hawk/Tornado package, but to a more stable and then less aggressive customer; the second development and more crucial for the United Kingdom to retain its position as a centre for combat aircraft design was renewed interest in a European collaborative advanced fighter. In 1978, meetings of British, French and German air staffs together with their defence ministers proposed a joint ECA. This timely intervention further underlined the risks, industrial and political of depending upon domestic requirements and the dubious attractions of an export-led development programme. Europe, for all its complications, was again offering a less precarious way forward for the UK military aerospace industry.[69]

Initial talks on the ECA proved to be a false start when it proved impossible to produce 'an affordable harmonious solution to ECA'. However, in 1983, the RAF revaluated its requirements to emphasise air superiority. This formed the basis for bilateral discussions with the German Air Force, which were expanded later that year to include France, Italy and Spain, leading to an Outline European Staff Target in December 1983. In July 1984, the five defence ministers agreed to a six-month technical and industrial feasibility study of a joint fighter aircraft programme.[70]

From the outset, there were critical differences between the 'British' and French design concepts. The United Kingdom wanted the extra range and weight implied by twin engines – the 'twelve tonnes' concept. The French preferred a much lighter design of '8.5 tonnes', which would also be compatible with carrier operations and as a cheaper design, be more attractive as an export vehicle. The Germans also preferred the lighter aircraft. The heavier design

---

[68] Letter from BAe Chairman to Prime Minister, 21st September 1981, NA FCO93/2669; Notes of Foreign Secretary's visit to BAe, 8th September 1981, NA FCO93/2669; Notes of MoD sales tour to Middle East, 16–17th August 1981, NA FCO93/2669; Letter from Prime Minister to King of Jordan, 30th March 1981, NA FCO93/2669; Minutes of meeting between MoD and German MoD, *Sales of Collaborative Projects*, 27th March 1981, NA FCO93/2669.

[69] *A Future Fighter Aircraft for the RAF; Consideration of the Options*, Paper by Ministry of Defence Equipment Policy Committee, 2nd April 1985, NA DEFE72/411.

[70] Ibid.

would also require a more powerful engine solution, reflecting Rolls-Royce's plans. At an industrial level, although some of the bitterness created by the AFVG experience had dissipated, there were still serious differences between the British and the French companies. However, while BAe and Dassault differed over 'leadership' concepts', the engine proved again to be the source of most of the industrial problems. The French wanted the aircraft much later than either the British or the Germans – a view that was interpreted as wanting to protect continued sales of the Mirage 2000. In general, the United Kingdom felt that the French had the objective 'of placing themselves in a strong position to dictate the terms of any possible collaboration'.[71] 'Here the French have the enviable evidence that their aerospace industry operates form a position of well-coordinated national strength and with form popular and political support.' This was well demonstrated by the high level of attendance at the airshow. They also had some confidence that they would be able to sweep up the Germans into 'their combat aircraft camp rather than ours'.[72]

In December 1983, the British, German, Italian and French Air Forces issued a draft European Staff Target calling for an aircraft of between 8.5 and 9 tonnes, a clear compromise between the French and British positions. However, the engine issue had if anything become more difficult, and closely tied to the respective interests of Rolls-Royce and Snecma. Rolls had developed a comprehensive business plan across all its engine operations, civil and military, emulating the integrated approach of its American competitors. The MoD was willing to back a new family of military designs in an eight-year programme worth £329 million. The combined effect of this integrated approach to all engine development ensured that Rolls-Royce was 'out on its own in Europe', a view that tended to view Snecma's capabilities with some-thing close to derision. The only issue that appeared to unite the French and the British was their concern that German arms transfer polices might hamper exports of any joint programme.[73]

The engine question had, in fact, become a two-part issue. The production EFA would require a new engine, but in order to move more rapidly and cheaper towards a final product, the prototypes would ideally benefit from an interim engine. The British suggested the Rolls/Turbo Union RB.199 power-ing the Tornado. The French preferred a version of the General Electric GE.404. The RB.199 was a better fit for the EFA and would be a good

---

[71] Record of MoD visit to France, 20th May 1983, NA DEFE71/1108; MoD Memorandum, 18th May 1983; MoD Minute, 10th May 1983, NA DEFE71/1108.

[72] Ibid.

[73] MoD Note, *Engine Aspects of EFA*, 26th March 1984, NA DEFE24/2983; MoD Memoranda, 19th June 1984 and 11th June 1984, NA DEFE24/2983.

performance match for the final specification. Fitting the GE.404 would require a different fuselage configuration, affecting the ultimate EFA design. Using the RB.199 would also enable the development of a demonstrator for the final engine, cutting technical risk and reducing total costs. The RB.199 was an important industrial asset to Rolls and extending its life would be of considerable benefit. The British Industry Secretary Norman Tebbit was keen to launch a new Rolls engine and using the RB.199 in the prototype was an 'obvious' choice. This was already far superior to any the French could offer: 'This', he wrote,

> 'points to an engine solution which recognises RR's technological lead in Europe. Snecma is not in the same league, the Americans having deliberately and systematically avoided giving them the sort of hot end technology that only RR has in Europe. Some technology transfer cannot be avoided if European military engine collaboration is to be fostered. But I believe it should only be fostered in a way which recognises full the technological and industrial realities of the current situation.'

Heseltine warned that there was a danger of the 'engine tail wagging the aircraft dog' and losing a huge potential market. Indeed, the issue could be the 'break point for the negotiations'. He sympathised with the industrialists' standpoint, but 'the real world was that he was in the business of furthering European collaboration which he regarded as a valuable to secure an effective European defence industry capable of taking on the Americans or collaborating with them'. But finally, he agreed to press the case for the RB.199.[74]

In line with a thread in UK aerospace policy since the mid-1960s, the interests of Rolls-Royce were again a key concern for the United Kingdom. However, in this instance BAe was largely supportive not only of developing a new engine but also of the 'hybrid' approach. This would maintain the momentum of development and minimise delays in production to beyond 1995 that would harm the BAe but even more so the avionics industry. There was, according to Sir Ray Lygo, chairman of BAe, 'little incentive to Dassault to come in on time'. He concluded that work on a national option would 'keep up the pressure for genuine collaboration and to have a fall-back position'.[75]

If the engine issue was the major source of tension, UK officials were also aware the French government was as much concerned about Dassault as Snecma. In June 1984, a French official told his UK MoD colleagues that the

---

[74] Letter from Secretary of State for Industry to Secretary of State for Defence, 10th August 1984: Meeting between senior executives of Rolls-Royce and BAe and the Secretary of State for Defence, 11th July 1984, NA DEFE24/2983.

[75] Letter from Chairman of BAe to Secretary of State for Defence, 19th July 1984, NA DEFE24/2983.

'real reason for the French stance was the industrial impact the EFA would have on Dassault'. Their demands for a larger workshare based on national uptake and export performance stemmed directly from Dassault's current workload and would find it hard to accept that future exports would have to be shared between five nations. France also wanted its own production line, presumably to facilitate its own export share – which might in any case be the norm for all the partners. Equally, going it alone would leave the company facing European competition for the first time in decades. This position was unacceptable to the United Kingdom and probably the three other partners. Overall, the MoD was left with the impression that the French had done 'a good deal more homework than us in assessing the industrial impact of EFA'. Presciently, the MoD observed, 'this may lead them to conclude that they would be better off going it alone (no doubt after prolonging negotiations sufficiently to give the Mirage 2000 a clear run into the mid-1990s)'.[76]

The five-nation National Armaments Directors (NADS) meeting, which preceded the Madrid Inter-governmental in July 1984, recommended a twin-engined 9.5 tonne design, with a new advanced technology engine, and an interim engine for the prototypes. The Madrid agreed to a full-scale industrial feasibility study based on a 9.5 tonne aircraft but failed to agree on a formal project launch. The Panavia group inevitably suggested an industrial organisation reflecting their experience; Dassault wanted a classical single company 'design leadership' formula and described the Panavia option as 'inviting us like a turkey to a Christmas dinner'. Heseltine noted that both the French and the British were being 'briefed' by their respective aircraft companies, and in passing he said, 'We are seeing a re-run of the balancing of interests between the British and French industry which had been a feature of the last 20 years.' The United Kingdom made several concessions in design to reach this interim agreement, notably overweight, which implied a smaller aircraft with a more limited radius of action and a less effective radar system. This suited France and Germany, as they required a 'Central European Front' aircraft while the RAF was looking to operate from UK bases. Ultimately, the French wanted a cheaper and thus more 'exportable' design, as a British official noted in the summer of 1984: 'French influence will tend to subdue UK ambitions on size, and this will undoubtedly help in rendering the aircraft more saleable.'[77]

---

[76] Defence Sales Organisation, *European Fighter Aircraft*, 28th August 1984, NA DEFE24/2983.

[77] MoD Note of Madrid EFA Intergovernmental meeting, 13th July 1984, NA DEFE24/2983; Letter from Secretary of State for Defence to Prime Minister, 19th July 1984, NA DEFE24/2983; Claude Carlier, *Marcel Dassault; la legende d'un siecle*, Paris, 1992, pp. 516–19; Defence Sales Organisation, *European Fighter Aircraft*, 28th August 1984, NA DEFE24/2983. This perhaps summarised the long-term dilemma in UK military aircraft procurement since the late 1950s.

By the end of 1984, Heseltine's optimism about moving forward on the EFA was threatened by a hardening of French attitudes. The British embassy in Paris reported that Dassault had written to both the French president and the prime minister, effectively asserting that five-nation collaboration could not be 'made to work'. Evidently, Marcel Dassault had intervened personally to press France to abandon multilateral cooperation. However, the real stumbling block was the 'whole question of engines'. Some in the MoD were now convinced that 'the long-term aim of the French is apparently to proceed with the M.88 and to engineer a break-up of the international dimension (with France as the innocent party) such that the definitive power plant will be the M.88'.[78] An MoD official went further, describing dealing with the French on the engine question as:

> 'We were in an almost constantly in a bizarre Alice in Wonderland situation in which it is virtually impossible to have a sensible discussion.' The French were fundamentally ignorant about 'hot end' technology but matched only by 'surpassing self confidence that they are actually masters of the subject. The fact that their claims are explicitly contradicted by their very limited technical achievements does not deter them in the least from advancing the most forthright, generally critical of the UK, and at the same time ill-founded opinions. One might well imagine that the French had developed the RB211 and RB199 and that we had struggled for 17 years with the M53'.[79]

This was part and parcel of a relationship going back to before Concorde, and despite Rolls bending over 'backwards' to satisfy French interests, the United Kingdom was still 'struggling for an accommodation with Snecma'. He concluded that as the world leaders in military engines, the Americans would view with 'derision the approach advocated by the French'.[80]

The engine question was now *the* issue. The United Kingdom was as eager to promote its industrial interests as the French. Part of the hesitancy in accepting the all-new engine approach was a fear that too much technology would help French engine ambitions to put Snecma into the 'big league' of world engine manufacturers. This would undermine Rolls-Royce and its ambitions to 'make itself independent of launch aid (for civil projects). The adverse implications for the UK could well be profound'. The interim engine approach would allow the United Kingdom to maximise its investment in earlier engines and help Rolls to use this as the basis for further business. The MoD also noted that the Americans had taken great care to isolate the French from anything of direct value to their military needs. However, the MoD felt that the United Kingdom could use this

---

[78] Letters from UK Embassy Paris, to Ministry of Defence, 11th January 1985 and 30th January 1985, NA DEFE72/408; MoD note, 30th January 1985, NA DEFE72/408.
[79] MoD Memorandum, 10th January 1985, NA DEFE72/498.   [80] Ibid.

to bolster their overall position in the negotiations, as the French would be left with 'a major problem without an obvious solution' – a belief that French options on a suitable engine were limited. Rolls-Royce also had the possibility of working with the United States, probably P&W on future military engines. Officials also noted that any weakness on the part of the other EFA partners on the engine question could be countered with reference to the strength of the British engine industry and the benefits that could accrue from the British strategy.[81]

Not for the first time, Rolls' balancing act between European interests and the lure of links with US industry were apparent. The pressure on the UK government to defend Rolls-Royce's position intensified with the news in April that Derby was drawing closer to P&W in both civil and military aero-engine development. The MoD believed that Rolls had tried hard to work with its European partners, especially the French, but after twelve months of negotiations there had been little progress on most of the core issues, from work sharing to fundamental design principles – 'Any one of these points would constitute a significant obstacle to progress. In aggregate they represent a serious problem.'[82] Although very tentative at this stage, P&W was also interested in cooperating with Rolls on military engines centring on the XG40 demonstrator, which appeared to complement P&W's large military engine work. Further cooperation could build on existing joint work on the Pegasus, developing jointly a replacement engine for a future VSTOL programme. Crucially this would be collaboration 'between equals'. Moreover, it was seen as significant that P&W had been 'making the running'. Rolls-Royce would further benefit from American industrial efficiency – 'a lesson they will not secure in Europe'.[83] The French firm had been entirely open about its ambitions, aims emphasised by Snecma's insistence on taking responsibility for the high temperature segments of the design. This would enable them to 'leapfrog' into a new generation of engines that Rolls has taken fifteen years to achieve – 'left to their own devices the chances of Snecma succeeding in such a major jump must be negligible'.[84]

The French too were now clearly moving to a national beat. The MoD was also aware that senior Dassault figures were increasingly opposed to a five-nation programme and that France would derive more benefit from a national

---

[81] Ministry of Defence Memorandum, *EFA Propulsion: The American Influence*, 1st April 1985, NA DEFE72/410; MoD position paper, 5th February 1985, NA DEFE72/409; MoD note, 5th February 1985, NA DEFE72/409; Telegram from British Embassy in Rome, 7th February 1985, NA DEFE72/409.

[82] Ministry of Defence Memorandum, *EFA Propulsion: The American Influence*, 1st April 1985, NA DEFE72/410.

[83] Ibid.   [84] Ibid.

programme. They were looking beyond the European theatre to focus on wider export markets. The French government was fully behind the M.88 engine and a French engined Dassault prototype could be flying by 1990. This reality was summarised in a letter from Heseltine to Mrs Thatcher in February 1985: the Panavia group were agreed about the design, but the French were now clearly the outliers, and a five-nation collaboration would only be achieved on French terms. He felt that there should be no 'winners and losers' because of collaboration. But it would 'require a conjunction of political will at the highest level to achieve this'. In general, the debate was at heart an Anglo-French issue, but the United Kingdom could not take the Tornado political alliance as necessarily guaranteeing the outcome in Britain's favour.[85]

At the same time, both the national technology demonstrators, the EAP and the ACX, were progressing; but while the latter was being shaped as the basis for a national French production programme, the EAP was not seen as a British equivalent. Heseltine explained that this would be 'some 15–20 per cent dearer' and the United Kingdom would forgo 'the potential benefits in terms of defence and wider political cooperation which a project of this size would be enormous'. He was still hopeful of working with the French, who appeared to be affected by a 'lack of experience in, and hence suspicion of, a major aircraft collaboration involving several partners'. BAe was willing to accept Dassault leadership, but Rolls was not prepared to concede much to Snecma. From a British perspective, the most promising development was that the German government was tending towards a four-nation solution.[86]

By the summer of 1985, the five-nation EFA was dead in the water. At the Le Bourget air show in June, the ACX, now officially described as the Rafale prototype, was pitted directly against the EAP and the EFA concept. The Germans were now firmly in the EFA camp. A final meeting between Heseltine and Hernu failed to bridge the gap and he was being hounded by Norman Tebbit to reach an agreement that would end the stalemate in favour of UK industrial interests.[87] In August, the United Kingdom, Germany and Italy met in Turin to finalise a draft agreement on the EFA. Spain delayed full membership until September, but effectively the Tornado group would form

---

[85] Letter from Secretary of State for Defence to the Prime Minister, February 1985, NA DEFE72/409; MoD report of visit to France, 12th February 1985, NA DEFE72/409; Note of meeting between Secretary of State for Defence and Minister for Information Technology (DoI), Geoffrey Pattie, 20th February 1985, NA DEFE72/409.

[86] Letter from the Secretary of State for Defence to the Prime Minister, March 1985, NA DEFE72/411.

[87] Telegram from British Embassy in Bonn, 14th June 1985, NA DEFE72/412; Letter from Secretary of State for Industry to Secretary of State for Defence, 14th June 1985, NA DEFE72/414.

the basis for what would become the Eurofighter consortium, with a matching industrial group EuroJet formed to develop the engine.[88]

The British embassy in Paris, perhaps best place to judge the interplay between the United Kingdom and France, recorded a view, if partisan, of events. Dassault was seen to have been running an extensive press campaign denigrating BAe's capability, pouring scorn on the Tornado's export record, and playing up the 'success' of Franco-German collaboration. Dassault was

> [f]ighting from the very outset for high stakes, outright leadership of the European fighter aircraft industry. They hoped to crush their main European rivals BAe, they showed little sign throughout the negotiation of any willingness to compromise. Their strong hold over the French media was matched only by their skill in manipulating the rest of the French aerospace industry and the French Government into accepting that vital French technology, independence and jobs were threatened by the proposed merger of Europe's industrial effort to build a fighter aircraft.[89]

The prior history of the difficult relationship between Britain and France over military aerospace cooperation since the mid-1960s would have made collaboration on EFA difficult. Although relations between BAe and Dassault had improved since then, some of the old issues were as before. The international consortia form of programme management might have diluted 'Leadership', but there were still key questions of design philosophy and high-value work sharing to sort out, and the differences over engine technology remained as pernicious as ever.

There was one final major spat over industrial and technological choices, this time centring on differences between the United Kingdom and Germany over the Eurofighter's radar. Echoing the earlier dispute over Tornado equipment, the Germans wanted to use American Hughes technology as the basis for development, whereas the United Kingdom proposed a 'European' solution based on British concepts. Germany was no longer content to be the junior partner in collaborative projects and was determined to promote its own industrial and political interests. The debate was not helped by a growing financial crisis at Ferranti, the MoD's preferred UK candidate. This came to a head in 1990 with the takeover by GEC, and MoD guarantees to Germany over the performance of the British-designed ECR90 radar.[90]

---

[88] *EFA Weekly Report,* 2nd July 1985, NA DEFE72/413; Letter from Ivan Yates BAe to Secretary of State for Defence, 2nd July 1985, NA DEFE72/413; Note of NADS Meeting, 23rd July 1985, NA DEFE72/414.

[89] Letter from Defence Attaché Paris, to Ministry of Defence, 26th September 1985, NA DEFE13/1980.

[90] *EFA Equipment Selection, MoD Note,* 12th November 1985, NA DEFE13/1980; MoD Memorandum, *EFA Radar,* 3rd November 1989, AIR8/3913/2; Letter to the Prime Minister from the Secretary of State for Defence, 20th April 1990 NA AIR8/3913/2.

In some respects, France may have had the last laugh in the consequent Rafale versus Typhoon competition for world sales. The Eurofighter team started with the larger initial base market and where the cost of Rafale would be borne by one government. It is now clear, however, that the Rafale has drawn ahead in terms of export sales. The Typhoon was hampered by the late adoption of a 'look down' phased array radar, a result of budgetary constraints. Both have self-evidently generated wider industrial benefits, especially in the vital area of systems integration, engines and avionics. The unanswered and unanswerable question is how much better these returns might have been from one common European programme (and this is not to overlook Saab Grippen, where BAe acted as a design consultant on its Grippen programme). As we will now consider, this schism at the heart of European military aerospace has continued into the latest generation of combat aircraft, exacerbated by the United Kingdom's increased trans-Atlantic defence industrial links that began to flourish in the mid-1990s.

2 The Emergence of European Transnational Defence Companies 1980–2010

The focus so far has been on the trials and tribulations of the top layer of military aerospace programmes. We now turn our attention to the changing industrial structure of European defence beginning in the late 1980s. This was first discernible in the helicopter and guided weapons sectors led by the formation of distinct European multinational companies. However, in the 1990s, largely led by the United Kingdom, the European defence industrial environment was transformed by the creation of global *defence systems* companies, pre-eminently BAES but also Airbus, Leonardo and the guided weapons company MBDA. The United Kingdom, unusually for a major defence industrial producer, was especially welcoming to inward investment by American, French and Italian-owned defence companies. This followed the adoption a procurement system that encouraged competition for defence contracts as well as a liberal attitude to inward investment in key industries generally.

Airbus and the A400 M

Unquestionably, Airbus' challenge to the American dominance of ciivl aerospace manufacturing is *the* success of European Collaboration. This would require more space to recount than is available here. It survived several industrial and political crises, many caused by the UK government. Structurally it evolved from a classic project-based collaboration to produce a 'family' of airliners, in time winning independence from direct multi-government control, effectively becoming a European (now global) transnational company, also absorbing German Typhoon production and the Eurocopter group. It has production facilities in the four founding members, although the UK share of ownership lapsed with the sale of BAES' holding in 2005. As we will consider in section3, it is one of the big 'what ifs' of European cooperation why a military Airbus failed to emerge, although it might be already evident from the failure of the four-nation Eurofighter why this might have been difficult to deliver. Equally, despite its qualities as an airliner manufacturer, it was unable to solve the problem posed in developing a European military transport, the A400 M.

The A400 M began as an exemplar of 'traditional' project-based European collaboration involving the United Kingdom, France, Germany and several other European governments, which was inherited by Airbus Defence and Space in what proved to be an ill-judged fixed price contract. Its origins were in the protracted search for a 'Hercules replacement', an idea that Chris Gibson likens to the hunt for a 'DC-3 replacement' in the 1950s, a 'unicorn' concept that was eventually filled by another Hercules, the C-130 J. By the late 1970s, several European Air Forces were looking to replace either their fleets of Hercules or, in the case of France and Germany, the Transall. The United Kingdom had been looking at a series of design ideas since the early 1970s, but when the United States made it clear that it too was in the field, there looked like little point in taking on an American rival. In the event, the US requirement focused on a more strategic aircraft, which eventually became the C-17. This left the Europeans without an appropriate design, a gap that was filled in 1982 by Aerospatiale, BAe, MBB and Lockheed, who proposed the Future International Military Aircraft (FIMA) of 1982.[91]

Each participant came up with designs, most using the P&W STF-592 turboprop 'paper' engine. In the event, FIMA went through thirty different configurations with both jet and turboprop engines. The two final designs, however, fell between several conflicting requirements. After seven years of preliminary work, Lockheed left the consortium when it became clear that the USAF would not commit itself in advance to buying the aircraft. Casa and Alenia joined the now all-European group, now designated European Future Large Aircraft Group (Euroflag). From 1993 Euroflag continued to debate a multiplicity of alternative design concepts and engine solutions. By 1994, these had narrowed down to a design with four turboprops. As most of the Euroflag group were also members of the Airbus team, in 1995 programme

---

[91] Chris Gibson, *On Altas' Shoulders, RAF Transport Projects Since 1945*, Hikoki, Manchester, 2016, p. 252–3.

management was handed over to the newly created Airbus Military, ostensibly to bring Airbus' experience of commercial organisation and discipline to development. The aircraft was designated A400 M. The engine choice remained problematic with two European and one Canadian option on offer. All three were effectively new designs, albeit based on existing cores. The Canadian (P&W) design seemed the better fit, but in the event in 2003 political pressure led to the selection of a European design based on a Rolls-Royce core and developed by the Europrop International consortium (Rolls, Snecma, MTU and ITP).[92]

Launch politics were also affected by an Anglo-German competition to develop the A400 M wing, echoing a challenge that characterised many the later Airbus airliner projects. This threat was certainly a factor in the British government's support for the A400 M. The A400 M first flight was in 2009, but by then the cost of delivering the fixed price contract was causing serious financial problems for the Airbus Company. Tom Enders, the Airbus CEO, threatened to abandon the project. Airbus and the OCCAR contracting body agreed to re-negotiate the contract at a cost of €1.5 billion. The first operational A400 M was delivered to the French Air Force in 2013.[93] Meanwhile, Lockheed had begun a series of updates to the C-130, resulting in the C-130 J with a substantial British share, including the engine (Rolls-Royce Allison) and advanced technology propeller, flying in 1996 with the RAF as a launch customer. Delays in the A400 M also led the RAF to order both the C-130 J and the C-17. The result for Airbus has been a substantial fiscal drag on its overall performance and in general a poor advertisement for wider European military aerospace cooperation.

Helicopters and Guided Weapons

Two European helicopter groups emerged in the 1990s: Eurocopter (now part of Airbus) and Agusta-Westland. The former was based on the helicopter interests of MBB and Aerospatiale and collaboration on first the Tiger attack helicopter and then the NH-90 transport. The creation of Agusta-Westland was the final stage of the 'Westland' crisis of 1985–6. Westland had been struggling for some time and a bid from United Technologies/Sikorsky was challenged by the then Defence Secretary Michael Heseltine, who encouraged a 'European' alternative (although the UT bid also included Fiat). The deal with Sikorsky and Fiat went through. Heseltine famously walked out of the Cabinet over the decision, precipitating a political crisis that nearly brought down the Thatcher

---

[92] Chris Gibson, *On Altas' Shoulders, RAF Transport Projects Since 1945*, pp. 253–8.
[93] Ibid, pp. 258–9.

government. The 21 per cent share was large enough to give Sikorsky a 'close involvement in the day-to-day policy and practices' of the company. The partnership with the Americans (and Fiat) undoubtedly gave Westland a breathing space and saved some key technologies such as work on high-speed rotors.[94] However, in 1994 again facing deep financial problems, Westland was taken over by the British GKN. GKN, with its joint venture partner Finmeccanica (now Leonardo) turned Westland round. In 2004, GKN sold its share to Finmeccanica.

MBDA was one of the most successful corporate developments of the 1980s and 1990s. The company was based on a merger of the missile interests of BAe and Matra Defence in 1996. As one of the components of BAe, Hawker Siddeley and Aerospatiale had worked together on the Martel, an anti-radiation missile, in the 1960s. The Martel was arguably the most successful projects to have emerged from the 1966 Anglo-French military aerospace package. Matters were aided by a straightforward allocation of workshares reflecting the companies' expertise. The missile's modular design also facilitated individual national requirements. Over the next two decades there were other examples of European missile collaborative programmes, including the Franco-German MILAN and HOT anti-armour weapons. With lower development costs than a combat aircraft, France and the United Kingdom also launched several national programmes.

BAe had successfully fended off a major loss of business to the American Texas Instruments in 1983. The contract was for a defence suppression missile with the Texas Instruments HARM, a missile already in service with the United States, and the BAe/GEC ALARM, an all-new and on paper a technically superior option. The Treasury preferred the US solution, especially as Texas Instruments had lined up with Lucas to deliver the British HARM. The ALARM, however, would protect UK seeker technology, the 'brains' of several types of guided weapons.[95] Its loss would threaten any cooperation in the sector with the Americans and undermine Britain's ability to 'develop and manufacture complete systems' – an R&D programme alone (the Treasury's proposal) was not enough.[96]

In some respects, the Treasury's view proved accurate, at least in broad economic terms, as the ALARM did not sell outside of the United Kingdom.

---

[94] Cabinet Minutes, 9th April 1987, NA CAB/128/85/14; House of Commons Defence Committee, 1985–6, HC518, para. 129.

[95] 'A Defence Suppression Weapon for the Royal Air Force', Note by the Cabinet Secretary, 13th July, NA CAB/129/217/10; Cabinet Minutes, 21st July 1983, NA CAB/129/217/16, 26th July 1983, NA CAB/128/76/25, and 28th July 1983, NA CAB/128/76/26 and NA CAB/129/217/10.

[96] CAB/128/76/25.

However, the wider principle of supporting such a central defence technology was proven at least in the long term to have considerable value. Maintaining the electronics and software capabilities at Marconi, as well as the systems-integration skills necessary to design, develop and manufacture a complete weapons system was fundamental. Over time, the importance of guided weapons in general would, in many respects, become more marked than the platforms that carried them. In 1999, BAe absorbed Marconi Defence and Space, which was partnered with Alenia systems and in 2001 this became MBDA. In France, the state actively encouraged domestic rationalisation creating Matra Defence and the missile interests of Aerospatiale in 1999. MBDA's creation was in some respects a response to market pressures in the 1990s, as demand for missiles and guided weapons. The merger helped to protect both market share and its competence as a first-rate missile design centre. In 2012, MBDA merged with the German LFK company, creating a European transnational second only in world terms to Raytheon of the United States, which has also acquired several American missile companies, including Texas Instruments. In 2011, MBDA also acquired a US presence. MBDA also absorbed the missile interests of Airbus. MBDA is now owned by BAES, Airbus and Finmeccanica.[97]

MBDA is organised as a fully interdependent European transnational enterprise, with nationally located centres of specialisation. Crucially, MBDA has developed an unusually high degree of cross-border interdependence with specialisation of functions distributed across its various national subsidiaries. Although the British, French and Italian governments will contribute to R&D and procure its weapons, MBDA does not have a guaranteed set of national markets. Indeed, UK competitive procurement policies and the presence of Raytheon and other foreign-owned manufacturers in the United Kingdom allow some alternatives to MBDA. However, in general, MBDA has achieved a degree of integration on a scale equivalent to American companies. In general, MBDA's success has been built on the prior history of project-based collaboration based on Anglo-French expertise and demand. This was exemplified by the development of the Scalp/Storm Shadow cruise missile, which proved its effectiveness in operations in the Middle East. The strengthening of Anglo-French defence ties at a political level – 'The spirit of St Malo' – in the mid-2000s further aided the emergence of a fully integrated company. This helped to facilitate access to the fundamental research programmes funded by both governments as well as encouraging the economies of scale generated by guaranteed orders from Britain and France. This in turn helped to support the

---

[97] Renaud Bellais, 'MBDA's Industrial Model and European Defence', *Defence and Peace Economics*, 33:7, November 2022, pp. 876–93.

development of 'families' of products, sustaining activity through a succession of products.[98] In many respects, MBDA *should* be the archetype for European transnational military aerospace, but sadly perhaps, it still remains something of an outlier.

Globalisation

Individually, collaborative projects, as developed in Europe from the 1960s, were rarely administered in a cost-effective manner. National industrial and technological interests often dictated workshares and technical responsibilities. Perhaps the oddest of these outcomes was the production of Typhoon wings, left and right, in Italy and the United Kingdom. As we have already noted, there were fundamental clashes over engine and radar choices in the EFA/Typhoon and earlier in the AFVG. Although concepts such as 'design leadership' were diluted in the consortia forms that emerged with the Tornado, the French held on to the idea throughout the 1980s. Even the latter collaborative ventures such as the A400 M were beset by differences over engine choice and other requirements. The evolution of MBDA into a genuine European transnational company was something of an exception that threw other failed groupings into sharp contrast. MBDA was in many respects the kind of integrated European aerospace entity that had been anticipated in the early 1970s, but which never evolved beyond the ad hoc consortia.

By the late 1990s, the development of European aerospace, driven in large measure by military interests, took a different path towards 'globalisation', or at least in its initial and most distinctive form, 'trans-Atlanticisation'. Globalisation in this context means the creation or acquisition of overseas assets by a national firm – old hat in much of the rest of world manufacturing, but largely novel in the defence sector, which historically was closely aligned with national defence markets and national procurement systems. The disinclination, especially in the United States, to buy from an overseas manufacturer was caused by the political reluctance to spend national revenues on foreign products; to promote and defend national autonomy in development and production avoiding dependence on an outside source of supply; and to capture perceived 'spin-off' benefits from defence R&D and high-value employment. In most cases, governments were reluctant to allow foreign ownership of key defence industrial assets such as prime contractors and sources of core equipment and components such as engines and avionics.[99]

---

[98] Ibid.
[99] Keith Hayward 'The Globalisation of Defense Industries', in Richard Bitzinger, *The Modern Defense Industry*, Praeger, Santa Barbara 2009, pp. 107–22.

At the end of the Cold War, the world defence industry changed with remarkable rapidity. In the United States, the process of rationalisation, partly inspired by the so-called 'Last Supper' speech by the Defence Secretary, occurred quickly, leaving a small group of 'mega primes' and 'semi-primes' dominating the US defence industrial base. European defence firms, albeit at a slower pace, followed suit. These essentially domestic changes then began to assume a more explicit international dimension, a process that can be described at least in part as the globalisation of defence industrial activity. Globalisation in this context is more akin to the wider process of industrial change in civil manufacturing that began in the nineteenth century with the creation of multinational and then transnational enterprises.

The defence sector remained largely immune from these wider changes, with national defence companies supported by national governments. Overtime, as national security became more directly linked to industrial and technological security, defence production was increasingly subject to political control affecting ownership, relations with foreign companies and the export of goods and the transfer of technology. Equally important, defence production and weapons procurement became keyed into wider national political and bureaucratic processes. Indeed, a key distinguishing factor and a considerable barrier to entry for outsiders of the defence specialist companies has been their expertise in managing relations with military procurement agencies and government. This has usually entailed extensive lobbying operations directed at the executive and legislative branches of government. The advent of exotic platforms such as drones and the growing prominence of cyber and other information technologies, which the Western governments have sought, have not always been successful in encouraging the entry of these specialists into the defence business.[100]

The globalisation process is creating or accelerating the emergence of transnational defence markets and corporate structures. To some extent, 'national' defence industries, especially in Europe, have already been diluted by international collaboration; but the operation of international supply chains and foreign direct investment in national defence companies has increased the level of global integration. Globalisation has also been driven by governments trying to maintain competition in national markets by soliciting bids for key contracts from international suppliers. Finally, to meet the demands of new technologies associated with the Revolution in Military Affairs, governments and specialist defence companies will have to tap a wider global stream of

---

[100] Which they may be reluctant to do, deterred precisely by the bureaucracy associated with defence procurement, controls over their technology and poor rates of return on defence contracts.

innovation and perhaps also to change the way they do business, with a more flexible approach to procurement and the relaxation of specialised defence regulations. In particular, procurement agencies will have more easily fit in with more dynamic product cycles and demand for quicker return on investments.

Yet the extent of genuine globalisation at the prime contractor level was limited. The formation of EADS and BAES in Europe created two transnational defence primes; but only BAES can claim to be a global prime contractor with a significant presence in both the US and European defence markets and even its prime contractor status is still largely based on its role on the UK market position and its central place in UK government-negotiated European programmes. The US primes still have very few overseas assets or, by European standards, extensive networks of collaborative activity, an important exception being the Lockheed International F-35 partnership. There are, however, increasing flows of foreign direct investment in the defence aerospace industries, especially among supplier companies. Much of this investment is directed at the US market, motivated by the need to get round US barriers to the purchase of foreign weapons and to access US technology. Several American companies have 'recaptured' some of the foreign-owned assets in the US defence and aerospace market, especially Anglo-American holdings such as Smiths and Lucas Aerospace, the former by GE and the latter by Goodrich.

The defence industry globalisation resembles an iceberg, with much more significant activity below the surface. Further down the supply chain, the need to insert leading-edge commercial technology into defence systems has stimulated the globalisation process. So does an interest in capturing the assumed cost savings of commercial 'off-the-shelf' procurement and reducing the development time of major weapons systems. Many of these technologies and techniques are generated by commercial, often already multinational, companies operating in deregulated markets. To take one widely cited example, the embedded software in many weapons systems could come from anywhere in a global industry. National defence customers are increasingly dependent on global suppliers who have little incentive to conform to the political or bureaucratic requirements of specialised defence contracting. Much of this process is largely hidden from view and is outside formal political regulation.

The rapid globalisation of supply chains and the use of commercially developed technology is obscuring the national origins of many defence components and subsystems. Cash-strapped governments have mixed reactions to these developments. They want to increase the efficiency of defence contracting, perhaps through encouraging international competition, but they are also apprehensive about the implications of losing control over key industrial assets and core technologies. But if much of the globalisation process is occurring below the 'radar screen' of government concern or even visibility, then governments will have only limited ability to regulate the process, to control the flow of defence technologies or to maintain a role in defence industrial policy.

However, continuing concerns for national security and economic advantage may encourage governments to focus even more clearly on what they can see, and in areas they can do something about. There will be continued regulation – certainly in the United States – of mergers and acquisitions at the prime and high-level subsystems supplier level. But while the process of defence industry globalisation might be delayed, it cannot be stopped. The key question is how far the process can go without requiring a fundamental change in the relationship between governments and defence companies whereby firms are allowed to operate more freely in world markets but can expect less direct support for R&D and fewer political advantages in national markets.

Under these conditions, globalised defence firms are likely to behave like other transnational companies. National security considerations would continue to impose some constraints on their freedom to transfer technology, core manufacturing assets and, especially, systems-integration skills. In most other respects, however, globalised companies would make investment decisions based on market access and industry efficiency. Consolidated defence aerospace prime contractors would be even more motivated to source from an international supply base offering a cost-effective mix of world-class technology, best price and delivery times. In many instances, subcontractors would be linked to the primes in preferred-supplier agreements, trading long-term assured custom and participation in the design and development process for commitments to reduce cost progressively. At all points in the manufacturing system, companies would be searching globally for added value in both products and processes.

The domestic consolidation process has been driven by a belief that big is better and biggest is better still. Scale is important in building capacity to bear the financial and technical risks of being a prime contractor. It also increases the political critical mass – the better to manage customer relations and to influence the political process through mobilising the political and economic power of a large corporation. Horizontal integration provides the potential to capture a wider range of defence contracts, exploiting managerial skills transferable between different platforms. In some cases, the defence prime also has the potential to exploit vertical integration, winning profitable subcontracts and, with life cycle contracting increasingly popular, to take a large share of support and through-life business. The UK experience is especially relevant in this respect with the shift in BAe from a predominantly aerospace company to a generalised defence systems manufacturer.

British Aerospace (BAe) to BAe Systems (BAeS)

The globalisation of defence industrial activity, if not now just a British-led phenomenon, was certainly led by the United Kingdom, and reflected the transformation of BAe from a domestic, primarily, aircraft manufacturer into a global defence systems company. Given the long and troubled history of the UK aircraft industry since 1945, this transformation was remarkable. The forced mergers and rationalisation of the early 1960s had created two still relatively weak aircraft companies, BAC and HSA, in largely a nugatory attempt to retain a degree of competition in the sector. Both the Labour and Conservative governments had encouraged a merger between BAC and HSA between 1967 and 1974 (which had been recommended by two official reports into the industry). These failed, largely due to problems over valuation and the conflicting interests of corporate shareholders. Rolls-Royce's takeover of BSE ended a similar bifurcation in the engine sector, which markedly strengthened the company's ability to shape government policy towards aerospace (especially on the civil side). The creation of BAe as a nationalised firm in 1978 redressed this structural and political imbalance.[101]

BAe was not the first British firm to move into the US domestic market through acquisition. In 1995, Rolls-Royce bought the US Allison Engines, a major supplier of military turboprop engines to the Pentagon. In 1998, GEC-Marconi acquired Tracor, a major American defence contractor, for US$1.4 billion. At the same time, US defence and aerospace mergers, especially that of Boeing and MDD, was putting even greater pressure on European companies, especially those in the United Kingdom subject to external competition for major defence contracts. BAe had begun talks with the German DASA to create a European-based transnational, and in 1998, the two companies agreed in principle to form a joint company. However, GEC decided to sell its defence interests, which immediately attracted both French and, more ominously for BAe, American interest. In order to head off what was appearing to be a dangerous competitive threat, abandoning the link with DASA, BAe made a bid for GEC-Marconi in December 1998. The merger finalised in January 1999 created a vertically integrated defence systems company with interests in the United States and Europe. It also encouraged Aerospatiale and DASA to form EADS, which would become Airbus SA.

Compared to its state in 1989, the newly privatised BAe, while the largest MoD contractor, was poorly placed in world (i.e., the United States) rankings. But it was still in a better shape than its aerospace constituent parts of the 1960s

---

[101] Its civil division, although weighed down by poorly performing regional aircraft, also contributed significantly to profitability with the growing success of the Airbus.

and was developing several solid military aircraft platforms either independently or in cooperation with European and American partners. Its share in the Airbus, which was just beginning to make some commercial headway and on the verge of challenging the Americans with the launch of the A320, provided a growing source of revenue. The Al Yamamah deal with Saudi Arabia largely secured the immediate future of its military aircraft operation – further buoyed by the export success of the Hawk and the launch of the Typhoon. It acquired Royal Ordnance, the ailing Rover Cars, and a property broker. The latter two elements were later sold off, and BAe returned to its defence and aerospace core.

The real shift in BAe's perspective and balance as a 'British' aerospace company came in 1999, with BAe's acquisition of GEC-Marconi, a defensive takeover in the face of possible foreign competition inside the UK defence market. Collateral damage was the rejection of closer links with the European aerospace/defence industry – a strategic break that put the United Kingdom on a different trajectory to its European neighbours and erstwhile partners. This would be confirmed with the partnership to build the F-35 as the only Level One partner, with privileged access to design and development work. BAES sold its stake in Airbus in the early 2000s (in part to reduce its exposures to the civil business, but primarily to focus more sharply on its defence systems identity). But BAES still retains a share of the missile company MBDA.

BAe's American *demarche* had been preceded by Rolls-Royce's takeover of Allison a few years earlier. Not the strongest of the US engine companies, it had solid business with turboprops for aircraft such as the Lockheed Hercules. Rolls-Royce has turned this asset into a major source of revenue. Later acquisitions took Rolls into Germany and Singapore. This was not all defence work, but it has added to the globalised nature of the UK DIB. Other companies such as Smiths, Cobham, Meggitt and Martin Baker became insiders to the US DIB. By 2010, the United Kingdom had even won some concessions on the tough US controls over technology transfers through the Defence Trade Treaty. Combined with the inward investment aspect of the UK DIB, globalisation, especially its American dimension, still places the United Kingdom in a very different position to its European neighbours. Rolls-Royce is one of three world engine companies, also with a significant presence in the United States, and remains across the board the dominant European engine company. Snecma is part of the trans-European Safran equipment group. The result is likely to block the United Kingdom from further *European* developments in the aerospace sector, but it might conceivably increase the trans-Atlantic dimension of the UK industrial base.

Given the lead time of combat aircraft, it is perhaps not so surprising that the UK DIB has not changed markedly in this sector since the late 1980s. BAe, now

BAES Warton and Samlesbury, are still the primary centres for the design and manufacture of advance combat aircraft. While Tornado has come to the end of its life cycle, the Typhoon – just moving forward in the 1980s – is still in production and subject to a radar upgrade. Warton is also home to British UCAV development, based on an effective 'fast prototyping' team developed over the past ten years. BAES production facilities are regarded as world class and recognised as such by Lockheed Martin. Samlesbury is producing the rear sections of all models of the F-35; while not the most advanced part of the F-35, it is extremely rewarding in commercial terms. The Hawk is coming to the end of its lifetime. The Harrier and Nimrod were ended some years ago. The United Kingdom relies on the United States for maritime patrol aircraft and other specialist platforms. The international Tempest programme will thus be of increasing significance in maintaining UK competence in military aerospace.

Other European Industrial Structural Developments

Airbus, and its Defence and Space subsidiary, has also evolved from a politically inspired consortium, building one aircraft type into an independent global company with interests, primarily civil in the United States and China. It vies with Boeing to the world's dominant supplier of large civil airliners. The Airbus Defence and Space subsidiary has absorbed the Franco-German Eurocopter and the bulk of German aerospace production. Airbus is responsible for delivering the A-400 M, a military transport whose origins can be traced back to a 'NATO' concept in the early 1980s. The A400 M has had a troubled gestation, an extended development phase and a large increase in costs, now borne by Airbus as a fixed price contract with its sponsoring governments, including France, Britain, Germany and Spain. It is now partnering Dassault in the development of the Future Combat Aerospace System (FCAS), an uninhabited combat aircraft. Dassault remains outside of the European groups. It has had an interesting ownership history; a 20 per cent state shareholding in 1979 has passed through to Aerospatiale and then to Airbus but is now only 10 per cent of the shares in the aircraft company. Dassault still holds a privileged position in the French DIB and has prospered from rising sales of the Rafale and is determined to 'lead' the FCAS programme 'old style'.

The European rotary industry now comprises two European transnational firms: Airbus Defence and Space, which is largely a French and German core, and Leonardo Agusta-Westland. The latter merger followed the highly controversial Westland Affair of 1986, which might have seen Westland absorbed by Sikorsky of the United States. The rotary sector seems at present to be a sustainable duality, helped to some extent by a degree of type specialisation, but which might become less so over the next decade. Like the very effective MBDA, European helicopters are broadly competitive with US products. Leonardo has a significant investment in the United States. In this respect, the United Kingdom is thus no longer unique in posing trans-Atlantic connections, but it remains the leading exponent of globalisation in Europe.

Another Watershed?

Europe now has two ostensibly competing European advanced military aircraft programmes. This situation might have been avoided at the beginning of the century. The United Kingdom and France explored prospects for a joint UCAV programme, sharing mock-ups at successive Le Bourget and Farnborough shows. A new generation of BAES and Dassault personnel seemed to have put aside the history of dispute and rivalry. This led to the all-British *Taranis* demonstrator of 2006, which formed the technological starter for the *Tempest* programme. France also launched the six-nation nEUROn. Despite this faltering start, the British and French had another go at launching a joint UCAV programme in 2013 as part of a wider Cooperation Treaty. However, nothing substantive emerged – I suspect not entirely unrelated to BAES hesitation about sharing technology, especially low observables, that might attract US disapproval. The French also indicated a preference for working more closely with Germany. As the IISS notes: 'Once again London and Paris at the platform level were going their separate ways.'

The Tempest

The *Tempest* team includes BAES, Rolls-Royce, Leonardo, MBDA, Saab and several other key equipment suppliers. Over time the concept has moved from an uninhabited combat system to a fully fledged 'sixth-generation' fighter to replace the Typhoon in 2040. In this guise, it is officially designated the Future Combat Air System Technology Initiative. In December 2020, the British, Italian and Swedish governments sealed a MoU to work on a joint programme. In November 2021, the United Kingdom and Japan also signed a MoU on joint development of an advanced engine demonstrator that might be used on the *Tempest*. The MoU also included work on other UCAV-related technologies. The UK MoD has already committed £2 billion over four years to the project, aiming to launch full-scale development in 2025 for possible initial deployment in 2035.

The Tempest design concept is to employ wherever possible open architectures that will facilitate both continual upgrading and allow partner nations to develop and integrate their own requirements and equipment preferences.

BAES is also using advanced manufacturing techniques to reduce costs and give additional flexibility to future developments. Full development and production may cost over £25 billion. The design team also believes that the approach will both cut development time and keep costs to an affordable level. Parallel programmes will include 'loyal wingman' UAVs and advanced weapons with a fully networked capability. Crucially, the Tempest is from the outset conceived as an 'international' concept, detached from specific British or European requirements with export potential a fundamental goal. This will allow the partners scope to develop technology that can be transferred into other, national projects, such as Sweden's Gripen E. Japan's inclusion as a partner, if continued into full development and production would mark a major shift in its geo-defence industrial position; hitherto Japan has been a major partner/customer for American military aircraft. Japan is also working closely with Rolls-Royce on engine design that might power both the Tempest and Japan's own indigenous project, the XF9. Other collaborative activity includes work with MBDA on a derivative of the Meteor air-to-air missile.

The next step is for Japan to move into the next stage, full development and production, which will require a more substantial commitment of funds. Conformation of the partnership would go a long way to insure the overall affordability of the Tempest. It would signify a major shift in the axis of British military aerospace; although the programme has other European partners, an International Tempest would take UK aerospace away from the European base launched with the Tornado in the late 1960s. The Japanese would also break a long-standing link with US manufacturers, but their expectation is that the link with BAES will allow a much more extensive and liberal exchange of technology. BAES' experience and established track record as an open partner should help to smooth the creation of an effective partnership, but firm central management of the programme will be needed to keep costs under control.[102]

Japan's participation in Tempest was, now designated as the Global Combat Air Programme (GCAP) was confirmed in December 2022, with the aim of having the aircraft ready by 2035. Further cooperative activity will include work on a next-generation air-to-air missile. Joining the GCAP is potentially a step towards a higher level of military aerospace technological capability. Japan can bring advanced electronics and IT skills to the consortium as well as a proven competence in lean manufacturing. Combined with BAES' prowess in this area (a product of a link with Honda when BAe was also a car company), this promises a key to GCAP's long-term affordability. Adding Japan's likely

---

[102] 'The fighter jet that could create a new alliance between the UK and Japan', *Financial Times,* 27th November 2022.

order for the final product will also go a long way towards filling the gap left by Germany, now part of the Franco-German programme.

The final piece in the industrial jigsaw will be absorbing Japan into an effective collaborative culture. The Europeans have collectively experience of working with Japanese companies, and the latter have been loyal players in several American programmes. Equally important, the Panavia/Eurofighter culture ensures that BAES a more effective de facto leader of the programme, respecting the need for and value of a genuine sharing of technical and managerial responsibilities between the participants. This will entail all parties equal access to the 'noble work' of core technologies and systems integration. The politics of collaboration, and the need to absorb Japanese industry into a European collaborative exercise, will also demand sensitive handling. BAES, for all its undoubted experience and competence as a combat aircraft design centre, will not have the same managerial dominance as Lockheed Martin to control an international team. The United Kingdom does not wield the financial or market power of the Pentagon in shaping events. Indeed, financial weakness and uncertainty over future British defence budgets places Japan in a strong position withing the coalition.

The Future Combat Air System

The French-led, tri-national FCAS programme is falling behind schedule because two of the key members, Airbus and Dassault, cannot reach agreement on key design features. Dassault is responsible for the new fighter jet, while Airbus leads the 'loyal wingman' remote carrier drone design. Spain's Indra leads the sensor systems pillar, while Safran is building a new jet engine for the fighter. A major problem between the French and German partners has emerged over engine development and the sharing of intellectual property (IP). France appears reluctant to transfer IP to Germany and officials have generally disparaged German contributions to the programme. The two sides have yet to move beyond their tentative agreement, and of June 2023 had still to sign a firm contract. The major stumbling block appears to be Dassault's reluctance to share flight control systems technology. According to London-based defence analyst Francis Tusa, the French may be prepared if necessary to go it alone on FCAS, a sort of Rafale + domestic venture, launched on the continuing strength of Rafale exports.

In November 2022, the FCAS partners appeared to have resolved some of the problems obstructing progress. France, Germany and Spain reached an industrial agreement to take the FCAS project forward. The three governments agreed to a 'co-operative approach on an equal footing' 'under overall French responsibility'. The agreement broke the logjam that held up the programme amid what had been protracted industrial wrangling over workshare and technology sharing between Airbus and Dassault. The agreement paved the way for the start of the development of a demonstrator costing in the region of €3.8 billion. Dassault stressed that it had to be the clear leader in the development of the aircraft. This may not end the simmering dispute between the 'German' arm of Airbus and Dassault. Dassault is determined to retain tight control over core FCAS technology – prominently the guidance system – and Airbus is equally determined to access French propriety technology. The acid test will come with the transition from development to production.[103] Compared to the Tempest team, FCAS has not started well. The problems and tensions revealed during its launch might diminish as the programme moves forward. Much will depend on the relative strength of political support. The French are most obviously committed to a successful outcome – there is nowhere else for Dassault and other key suppliers to go over the next decade. It is a make-or-break project for the French military aerospace industry. German industrial options are similarly constrained. Although now buying F-35s, Germany is too late substantially to benefit from joining the F-35 team. The longer-term success of FCAS will depend upon exports outside of what is a limited bilateral market. This in turn might depend upon Germany further liberalising its defence export regime, which has been stretched by increasing commitments to sustaining Ukraine in its conflict with Russia. Time will tell if this will be extended to more challenging customers, particularly in the crucial Middle Eastern Market.

The prospects for a reconciliation of these two programmes are poor. It is hard to see as the development alliances mature and take up key roles in the respective programmes for an easy effective merger to be negotiated. The stability of neither cannot be taken for granted, but it is difficult to see how the key players in either the Tempest or FCAS could find a place in the others' programme. The fact that there are economic advantages in pooling the base market for the two aircraft is still a powerful incentive to broaden membership of a joint programme. However, with modern design and production techniques tending to lower the costs of some military programmes, this may be diminishing as a driver. There have been too many twists and turns in the history of European aerospace collaboration, but this may be the final watershed and an end to hopes of an integrated European military aerospace base.

---

[103] 'European fighter jet project moves into next phase', *Financial Times,* November 16th, 2022; 'Franco-German fighter jet projects still faces turbulence', *Financial Time,* December 30th November 2022.

3 Observations from Fifty Years of European Military Aerospace Collaboration

Ownership Issues

Over the years, the ownership of major European aerospace and defence companies has varied, but overall, the direct role of the state in European aerospace companies – especially in the civil sector – has diminished. It has gone completely in the United Kingdom and very much-reduced even in France. In the case of Britain, Rolls-Royce was nationalised in 1971 in order to resolve the bankruptcy crisis. BAC and HSA were nationalised in 1978 to form BAe, but both were privatised in the 1980s. Shorts was the only long-term exception – nationalised in 1944 to bail out an incompetent management. It was sold to Bombardier of Canada in 1989. Until the 1990s, and the transformation of Airbus into a largely privately owned company, most of the leading French firms were effectively state-owned. In the 1990s, the state reduced its direct role over firms such as Safran (including Snecma). Dassault was partially national-ised in 1979 following a managerial scandal, with systems business remaining as a family-held business. The state holding was later administered by Aerospatiale, which passed into Airbus ownership. This has been steadily reduced, leaving Airbus with a 10 per cent share of Dassault. The Italian government still holds a 30 per cent share of Leonardo.

However, the changing patterns of ownership have not reduced the political salience of nationally located companies or altered the fundamental politics of European military aerospace development. This has, for a few exceptional years in the case of the United Kingdom, placed Britain and Germany in principle on a different footing to France or Italy. In theory, this placed the governments of the latter group on a different footing compared to the former. Public ownership should imply a more direct line of funding and political support. However, this supposed advantage has been less detectable in the military sector. Undoubtedly, all the major European aerospace companies have a close relationship with their respective governments as primary cus-tomers, sponsors of programme development and providers of R&D funding. Indeed, the differences have often been more superficial than evident in terms of *outcomes*. In practice, major defence companies might be best described as *government-orientated enterprises*. In some cases, firms may be elevated to the status of 'national champions', with privileged access to public funds and an enhanced ability to influence government. The relationship between the French aerospace industry and the government has exhibited these character-istics to a more explicit extent to that of the United Kingdom: political, official and corporate elites have been interchangeable. Dassault, both as a company and through its charismatic founder Marcel Dassault, was an important contributor to right-wing political parties, including General de Gaulle while in domestic exile. This has afforded Dassault a continuing influence over French military aerospace policymaking.

British governments have taken, ostensibly at least in the recent, a more 'hands-off' approach to managing this relationship. Arguably, Rolls-Royce was elevated close to 'national champion' status during the 1960s; the 1971 bankruptcy was greeted as a national disaster as much as a corporate failure. The nationalised 'interlude' showed little change at an operational level (as did the short period of quasi state ownership suffered by Dassault in the 1980s). The main shift in the relationship was in the funding of civil projects when both Rolls-Royce and BAe were no longer eligible for repayable launch aid. Privatisation saw a return to this form of state-aided development, much to the chagrin of the UK Treasury that had hoped both companies might be weaned off dependence on state funding civil projects. It was 'crucial that BAe Plc be seen to stand on its own, independent of Government and wholly-free from Government control. The question of this principle would have to be satisfied before a specific claim on Government resources could be entertained'. BAe would be 'very rash to assume that the availability of launch aid is a foregone conclusion, and quite wrong to assume its availability in their assessment of the likely viability and profitability of the A320 project'. The Treasury, on the other hand, would not oppose something like a rights issue. However, the Treasury was disturbed by the publicity generated by BAe over the issue, as this seemed to be designed to put pressure on the government. The company must be made aware that the availability of launch aid would be, 'to say the least, problematical'.[104] Aerospatiale, on the other hand, as a publicly owned company always had access to equivalent French civil funding.

Although the early BAe senior management teams were not regarded in official circle as especially talented, the company's relations with the Thatcher administration steadily improved, especially after privatisation in the 1980s. The interaction between officials and companies, including secondment and transfer between government and industry service, might be more formally recognised in France than in the United Kingdom, but it nevertheless exists. BAe staff were 'embedded' in the MoD defence sales team and were prominent in negotiating both the abortive Iraqi deal and the Al Yamamah contract with Saudi Arabia. The latter going a long way to consolidate BAe's financial success. John Weston, later CEO of BAe, was seconded to the MoD to help promote the sale of military aircraft and he would be a member of the team that would eventually conclude Al Yamamah. In July 1982, he was established as 'the focal point' for the Tornado/P110 activity and the link

---

[104] Treasury Letter to Department of Industry, 13th July 1981, NA T457/28.

with BAe on these matters.[105] Indeed, French industrialists have often envied the effectiveness of the UK MoD Defence Sales Organisation.

The emphasis on 'competition' that emerged in UK defence procurement from the 1980s was less evident at the level of prime contractor, with neither BAe nor Rolls-Royce deprived of support for key programmes. The main effect of the policy was mainly felt further down the supply chain. More important than the competition policy per se was the increasing role played by foreign-owned companies in the UK defence and aerospace base. There was also an implicit understanding that as UK companies expanded their ownership of US firms in particular, the same rights of access should be extended to foreigners in the United Kingdom. This liberal approach to investment in strategic French industrial assets has rarely ben reciprocated with extensive barriers to inward investment in French defence and aerospace companies.

The more interesting issue is the extent to which the major players have benefitted from a coherent national strategy towards the domestic defence industrial base and a procurement policy that has encouraged the domestic product. In this respect, the French experience has been the most direct, with if not a formalised and continually refined DIB strategy, there has been a consistent pattern of industrial preference and support, including the determination of specifications that have favoured exports over domestic users. In the United Kingdom, user needs have held a much higher priority, although the formal organisation for export promotion has often been superior to its neighbours'. German industry, as well as its partners, for many years was hampered by a strict national policy towards arms sales. Finally, until very recently, UK industry has complained about the absence of a coherent national policy towards the DIB comparable to the French approach. It remains debatable whether this has hampered the overall success or failure of the British military aerospace industry. BAES has achieved a global spread that has probably been evenly achieved by its own efforts and by the support of successive British governments.

Collaboration and Competition

The balance of advantage and difficulty in collaboration was well argued in an MoD paper of 1975 – offering the military perspective on the forthcoming nationalisation of the aircraft industry.[106]

---

[105] FCO Telegrams, October 1981, NA FCO93/2669; Letter from UK Embassy Saudi Arabia, 27th September 1981; Letter to BAe from MoD Sales Organisation, 4th December 1981, NA FCO93/2671; BAe and the Defence Sales team were closely aligned during this periods, MoD letter, July 1982, NA FCO46/3238.

[106] MoD paper for Official Group on Aircraft Industry Strategy: The Military Aircraft Strategy, 15th January 1975, NA AIR8/2700.

The optimal position would enable a free and unconstrained choice of projects from domestic sources, but with an option on foreign supply where necessary. But freedom of choice was constrained by high R&D costs and long replacement cycles, and the costs of foreign procurement in terms of domestic employment and so on. Choice was between either collaboration or the end of domestic supply. The latter removed an ability to affect specifications and the timing of supply, and it created vulnerability to external factors, such as the Skybolt crisis of 1960. Over the long term, it left the United Kingdom vulnerable to a monopoly supplier and the loss of political influence attendant on export sales.

On the other hand, while

> 'Collaboration imposes some constraints on national requirements and pro-
> curement options, these are much less extreme than those that might arise
> from a total dependence on foreign purchases and the mutual reliance
> between partners which is a feature of collaboration provides its own guar-
> antee of support and enables British industry to maintain at least a partial
> capability in many areas which might otherwise have to be abandoned
> completely.'

There might be obvious exceptions such as large transport aircraft and special-ised AEW aircraft. Although the United States had shown more interest in cooperating with its allies, this was invariably on American terms. As a result, 'Collaboration with US was not generally desirable as it would be incompatible in the long run with maintaining even partial independent design capability.' European collaboration had the drawback of increasing costs, 'but efforts should be made to establish more permanent industrial arrangements with European partners, retaining a full capability within Western Europe but recog-nising the need for rationalisation of resources between partners'.[107]

The sentiments expressed in the 1975 MoD paper echoed those of the Unpublished Marshall Report of 1972, which stated that the government should take an active role in pushing for closer industrial cooperation and cross-border integration. More ambitiously, the end process should be the 'ultimate evolution of single dominating groups in both the airframe and aero-engine industries. But this might not be both universally accepted here or abroad, and the process will be in any event be slow and complex'. There was also a need to 'guard against a damaging polarisation of European industries into British and French led camps'.[108] As Minister for Aerospace from April 1972, Michael Heseltine was an early convert to the idea of a more comprehensive European solution, believing that integration was the only way to resist the 'American Challenge'. He strongly advocated the creation of two European transnational companies, arguing that ad hoc

---

[107] Ibid.   [108] *Review of the Aircraft Industry*, DTI, March 1972, pp. 5–9, NA T225/4315.

collaboration had led to a confused and potentially disruptive pattern. As he bluntly told the Cabinet, 'The UK interest in integration arises because the British national aircraft and engine industries are no longer viable.'[109]

In practice, a 'top-down', governmentally imposed rationalisation of the European aerospace industry melted away. In the United Kingdom, the arrival of the Labour government committed to nationalisation and domestic rationalisation pushed larger European moves into a political siding. At a European level, the French and Germans focused on building on the Airbus coalition on the civil side, a strategy that the United Kingdom endorsed in an official return to the programme in 1979. Military collaboration remained centred on another generation of ad hoc international programmes. By the 1990s, restructuring was left largely to the companies to sort out, with of course, some indirect political involvement.

Why a Military 'Airbus' Failed to Appear

The answer in part to this question is why the commercial Airbus in the end prospered. It was a struggle to say the least to get the consortium going and to survive over its first twenty years. This was very much the result of a strong political will on the part of the German and French governments to build a capability to take on American market dominance. There was no national alternative – a lesson that the British government initially failed to appreciate; but once American options were firmly rejected by BAe, the final piece fell into place. The maturing Airbus coalition was given an enormous boost by the huge success of one design, the A320, which still provides a massive contribution to Airbus revenues. There were tensions over work sharing amongst the partners, but these have largely been resolved under an increasingly firm centralised management. Finally, the supporting governments – WTO problems notwithstanding – proved willing to fund the development of a 'family' of products, with sufficient overall returns on investment to still criticism of 'subsidised' aerospace.

So why not a military Airbus? There was a similar political and industrial incentive to maintain an independent capability in the face of American competition and near-dominance of key military markets. There was some parity in core military aerospace technological capabilities, or at least the distance outside of some specific categories was close enough to support European ambitions. The absence of a fully integrated European market – the F-16 European customer base for example absorbed a key part of the European market in the 1970s – was one of the fundamental problems. However, Boeing still sold its airliners to Europeans, so this could not have been the sole cause of a European structural failure.

---

[109] 6th June 1972, T225/3788.

National industrial interests were clearly major issues; either French championing of Dassault and to a lesser extent Snecma or the United Kingdom and Rolls-Royce (the airframe sector was not quite as well defended) were persistent problems in launching a Franco-British 'European' core to the military sector. To some extent, the divisive force of British and French engine rivalry has lost its force. Partly Snecma, now part of the Safran group, may be losing the technical battle with Rolls-Royce with a continuing dependence on the future of FCAS and sales of the Rafale. Rolls, on the other hand, will benefit from work on the F-35B, although orders for the VSTOL 'B' version will be a fraction of overall sales of the F-35. Its future as a major military engine company will also depend on progress of the Tempest.[110]

Where Next?

Having been bitten early in my career with a confident prediction about the impending failure of the Airbus programme, I would not dream of launching into bold prophesies about the future of individual programmes, still less of the European aerospace industry. Table 2 shows that the United States remains by far the largest aerospace industry in the world.

There is self-evidently much at stake here. The sums involved in developing either *Tempest* or FCAS to squadron use are large and realistically beyond a single European nation. These might not deter France, used to ploughing a fiercely independent combat aircraft furrow, but they would certainly give the United Kingdom pause for thought. Even if the Ukraine crisis has made defence

Table 2 Major aerospace industries by employment (2021)

The US	**2,900,000**
France	**188,000**
The UK	**140,000**
Germany	**105,000**
Japan	**56,640**

Note: Data collected by national trade associations; criteria for inclusion are not consistent.

---

[110] Rolls-Royce, although one of only three global suppliers of advanced engines is by far the smallest of the three and under pressure to maintain its presence in civil markets. It may be increasingly vulnerable to a takeover by foreign owners, although this would be subject to UK government permission through a 'golden share' provision created on privatisation in the 1980s.

spending more fashionable again, affordability over the long haul is going to be of importance, especially given the United Kingdom's other expensive defence procurements. In passing, Ukraine has demonstrated the value of relatively cheap drones, in this case Turkish products used against the Russians.

We have yet to see the military effectiveness of the Tempest/FCAS proven by combat, and that is some years away. Before this is reached, there is the little matter of delivering very complex products to market on time. The Tempest, for the moment, as a piloted and larger vehicle, is the more challenging design. But both will cost several billion of pounds or euros to fully develop. Neither grouping of governments can afford to allow the programmes seriously to escalate in cost. They may also be fighting out for the same third-party sales. This might be eased by the likely restrictions on the sale of the next generation of US aircraft, but this may again be a rerun of the Rafale-Typhoon competition, with again a more expensive but arguably more capable 'British' product slugging it out with a relatively cheaper 'French' vehicle. Both will need these sales to extend production into profit; none of the governments are likely even together to establish a market sufficient to repay development costs. An accent on 'affordability' and a proven track record in manufacturing efficiency (both BAES and MHI) have some credibility in this respect. But the 'iron law' of learning curve costs implies that numbers in the end determine production costs and thus affordability to the customer.

Whatever the two 'competing' European projects might offer in terms of 'affordability' through internal productivity, the fact remains that Europe has yet again finished up with two broadly comparable projects aiming at similar military requirements. This has been the case now for nearly fifty years. The cast has changed – France and Germany pitted against the UK-based international coalition rather than two generations of French national projects matched by aircraft developed by the United Kingdom and Germany (plus Italy and Spain) – but the splitting of resources and market remains unchanged. One of the most important and potentially disruptive factors in terms of a common European approach to major military aerospace programmes remains the US-led F-35 programme, with the United Kingdom, Italy and others part of an international industrial team. BAES has a uniquely privileged design and production role on the programme, and British suppliers are responsible for up to 20 per cent of the aircraft. However, integration of MBDA missiles as an optional weapons' fit on the F-35 was achieved only after an industry campaign to ensure UK government support. But given that this is envisaged as a 'forty-year' enterprise, the F-35 is likely to dominate the top end of the fighter market for the foreseeable future. This affords the United Kingdom a significant production cushion and revenue stream, which over time is likely to surpass returns from an ageing

Rafale programme. In some respects, the European military aerospace industry has been left with two overlapping competitive forces – the continuing Typhoon/Rafale struggle, and the F-35 team (which has effectively divided the Eurofighter consortia).

The continuing fragmentation of Europe's military aerospace market, with three (now at least perhaps down to two) producing centres and several countries buying American products, reminds us of the most important economic truth that has provided an implicit liet motif for this study – the power of economies of scale and the learning curve effect. Put simply, the more aircraft built, the lower the unit cost of production. This is the learning curve effect: and as Sir George Edwards, one of the most powerful figures in British and European aerospace, was forever saying, 'we have had to live off the thick end of the learning curve', that is the United Kingdom (and Europe) had the same development costs of American companies but assured only a fraction of the initial sales they could confidently expect. This would also facilitate lower price offers to potential export customers, a key factor in civil sales but also valid for the military market.[111] While comparing advanced fighters is problematic (especially where different capabilities and generational factors are involved), the US F-16 has sold over 4,000 units, which exceeds the combined orders to date for the Typhoon, Rafale and Gripen. More telling perhaps, the base US order for the F-35 is some 2,500 and market estimates over the next thirty years (with upgrades) suggest total sales will be over 6,000. Conversely, fewer than 200 F-22s have entered USAF service, making it the most expensive fighter in service in terms of unit costs; but it is the most technological fighter aircraft currently in operation, a premium that the United States can and will pay for superiority.

Sadly, a fully integrated European military aerospace sector is the less likely outcome of the FCAS/Tempest programmes. Nor, it should be said, that the European defence market is likely soon to possess the same (protected) coherence of the United States. Italian and Swedish involvement in the *Tempest* might to a degree simplify the European military aerospace industrial tapestry, but this is still far short of the kind of rationalisation that could underpin a more collective European effort. Nor would I bet against a possible linkage between at least one of the European players, continuing F-35 cooperation into the next generation of combat aircraft. This may not involve the same depth of cooperation on the emerging sixth-generation projects in the United States as on the F-35; but given a half decent technical or process-related competence to barter

---

[111] This advantage was cruelly exposed in 1965, when the TSR-2 was matched against the price offered to the UK for the F-111 that was initially ordered as its replacement.

with the Americans, this option cannot be ruled out. Problems with divergent requirements or unsynchronised military/budgetary timescales continue to create difficulties for the military sector. The A400 M was probably the worst case of divergent requirements, different in national industrial interests and timing. Finally, the temptation either to buy American or to join forces with a US programme has been a persistent factor, especially in British choices. In particular, the spectre of the F-35 has, and will continue to, cast a long shadow over European military aerospace, offering a powerful alternative to existing ECA, and with regular upgrades, an attractive choice for the foreseeable future.

In some respects, the somewhat facetious view that European military aerospace development and production has perhaps remained fundamentally unchanged since my 1969 undergraduate essay has some validity. The civil aircraft side has undoubtedly undergone a highly successful transformation; in some respect, Airbus is now *the* dominant player in the civil market. The military sector is still waiting a similar transformation. Even the United States has seen the number of design centres for bombers and fighters drift towards single contenders. And when there is scope for competition, losing contenders are often awarded significant amounts of subcontract work. Europe still lacks a workable collective defence industrial policy; and with the United Kingdom outside the EU political framework, it is hard to see an easy way to include the British in either formulating or implementing such a collective approach to delivering a such a policy.

Realistically, the future is more likely to resemble the past; a partially integrated European military aerospace industry struggling against rising costs to stay in touch with the United States. My personal view is that a major opportunity was lost in the 1980s with the failure to include France in what became the Typhoon coalition. The reasons were, as we noted in Section 1, largely the product of national industrial interests that harked back to the 1960s rather than looking forward to a new generation. There always seemed room in the defence business for a less than optimal collective solution. There were never quite the same commercial pressures equivalent to the centrifugal forces driving the Airbus partners in an effective industrial answer to the Americans. After nearly seven decades of European military aerospace collaboration, this must be regarded as a disappointing outcome. Paradoxically, the United Kingdom might be better placed than most of its neighbours, linked to two international coalitions, one the US-led egg firmly basketed and a Euro-Japanese alliance in the making for the future. Compared to 1964, this is a far healthier position for its combat aerospace industry. In this sense, salvation has come through collaboration, even if not quite in the direction first envisaged.

Select Bibliography

Bitzinger, R. (ed.) (2009). *The Modern Defense Industry*, Santa Barbara: Praeger.

Gibson, C. (2019). *Typhoon to Typhoon: RAF Air Support Projects and Weapons since 1945*, London: Hikoki Publications

Hartley, K. (2014). *The Political Economy of Aerospace Industries*, Cheltenham: Elgar.

Hartley, K. (2019). The political economy of arms collaboration. In R. Matthews, ed., *The Political Economy of Defence*, Cambridge: Cambridge University Press.

Keith, H. (1989). *The British Aircraft Industry*, Manchester: Manchester University Press.

Meijer, H. and Wyss, M. (2018). *The Handbook of European Defence: Polices and Armed Forces*, Oxford: Oxford University Press.

Olsen, J. A. (ed.) (2018). *Routledge Handbook of Air Power*, Abingdon: Routledge.

Cambridge Elements ≡

Defence Economics

Keith Hartley
University of York

Keith Hartley was Professor of Economics and Director of the Centre for Defence Economics at the University of York, where he is now Emeritus Professor of Economics. He is the author of over 500 publications comprising journal articles, books and reports. His most recent books include *The Economics of Arms* (Agenda Publishing, 2017) and with Jean Belin (Eds) *The Economics of the Global Defence Industry* (Taylor and Francis, 2020). Hartley was founding Editor of the journal *Defence and Peace Economics*; a NATO Research Fellow; a QinetiQ Visiting Fellow; consultant to the UN, EC, EDA, UK MoD, HM Treasury, Trade and Industry, Business, Innovation and Skills and International Development and previously Special Adviser to the House of Commons Defence Committee.

About the Series

Defence Economics is a relatively new field within the discipline of economics. It studies all aspects of the economics of war and peace. It embraces a wide range of topics in both macroeconomics and microeconomics. *Cambridge Elements in Defence Economics* aims to publish original and authoritative papers in the field. These will include expert surveys of the foundations of the discipline, its historical development and contributions developing new and novel topics. They will be valuable contributions to both research and teaching in universities and colleges, and will also appeal to other specialist groups comprising politicians, military and industrial personnel as well as informed general readers.

Cambridge Elements ≡

Defence Economics

Elements in the Series

A full series listing is available at: www.cambridge.org/EDEC

Printed in the United States
by Baker & Taylor Publisher Services